How Assessment Supports Learning

Hong Kong University Press thanks Xu Bing for writing the Press's name in his Square Word Calligraphy for the covers of its books. For further information, see p. iv.

How Assessment Supports Learning

Learning-oriented Assessment in Action

David Carless
Gordon Joughin
Ngar–Fun Liu
and Associates

香港大學出版社
HONG KONG UNIVERSITY PRESS

Hong Kong University Press
14/F Hing Wai Centre
7 Tin Wan Praya Road
Aberdeen
Hong Kong

ISBN   978-962-209-823-7

British Library Cataloguing-in-Publication Data
A catalogue record for this book is available from the British Library.

Secure On-line Ordering
http://www.hkupress.org

Printed and bound by Pre-Press Limited, Hong Kong, China.

Hong Kong University Press is honoured that Xu Bing, whose art explores the
complex themes of language across cultures, has written the Press's name in his Square
Word Calligraphy. This signals our commitment to cross-cultural thinking and the
distinctive nature of our English-language books published in China.

"At first glance, Square Word Calligraphy appears to be nothing more unusual than
Chinese characters, but in fact it is a new way of rendering English words in the
format of a square so they resemble Chinese characters. Chinese viewers expect to
be able to read Square Word Calligraphy but cannot. Western viewers, however are
surprised to find they can read it. Delight erupts when meaning is unexpectedly
revealed."

— Britta Erickson, *The Art of Xu Bing*

Contents

Foreword

Why bother with assessment? Surely, examinations have been a successful strategy for endless years, we are familiar with them and they have helped us get where we are today. Students may find them challenging, but they have served us well. This is often the starting point when trying to open discussion about assessment in higher education. Assessment is defined by past practice, not by what it is needed for now.

There are many reasons why we need to revisit some of our taken-for-granted assumptions about assessment. Not only are we seeking to extend the range of outcomes for higher education courses beyond what can be assessed in examinations, but the student population is getting more numerous, more diverse and more demanding. This is as true in Hong Kong as it is in most countries with an expanding system of higher education.

Thinking afresh about assessment is not a simple matter, as we tend to think in terms of our own educational experience, what has worked for us and what we feel comfortable with doing. However, just because examinations may have served us well does not mean that they are suitable as the exclusive diet for our own students. Luckily, many of our colleagues have been engaging with this problem and there is an increasing range of ideas that have been tested in practice to guide us into new directions.

This book provides ready access to some of these ideas and practices. It provides a useful starting point for exploring what is available and what might be used in different situations. Most importantly, it reports many examples from different disciplines, all within the Hong Kong context. It provides a robust rejoinder to those who read about new ideas from overseas and think that they could not be used here with our students. This book shows that not only can they be used here, but also there are further innovations being generated to meet the needs of local circumstances. It is clear from the contributions that Hong Kong is in the forefront of assessment innovation in higher education.

This book is not just a collection of interesting examples of what works in assessment practice. It is also a good guide to the fundamental shift in assessment thinking from a belief that assessment is just about measuring student performance to one that recognizes that assessment is a powerful influence on learning and must be judged in terms of its influence.

The project from which the book arose focused on what the authors have termed learning-oriented assessment. This is not just a new piece of educational jargon, but also a signal of the important shift in assessment thinking. It represents the need to think of all assessment practice in terms of the impact it has on student learning. Assessment is not just a measurement that leaves the student untouched, it is a strong intervention into their world of studying and it points students to what is important and what they should be doing. It changes their behaviour more readily than anything else we may do in our teaching.

Assessment can be regarded as an act of teaching. It teaches students what we value, what we require of them and what they must emphasize if they are to satisfy us. It is an act of communication that guides their path as surely as anything else we do. Seeing assessment as an act of teaching is not enough. We must also see it as an act of learning. Students must learn from assessment activities what we want them to learn. Unfortunately, there is plenty of evidence that not only do they not learn what we want, but also they learn to do things that are very disadvantageous. There is ample research to suggest that they memorize without understanding, they reproduce without internalizing and they can appear to solve problems without appreciating the underlying conceptions on which their solutions are based.

We therefore need to engage with new ideas about assessment to avoid falling into these traps. It is timely that we do so now as the demands of assessment are increasing, as the number of students whom we assess seems to increase every year. The challenge we face is to think smartly about assessment so that we can improve the quality of student learning without increasing the burden on staff.

Learning-oriented assessment is about placing learning as the foremost consideration in assessment practice. This does not mean ignoring the role of assessment in certification, but ensuring that learning is considered every time assessment is mentioned. This book provides a vital stimulus to this task. It shows how assessment can be used to improve learning, it increases the repertoire of activities that can be used for this purpose, and it contextualizes this within academic disciplines and the local context. It is a pioneering book that should be taken up widely.

David Boud
Professor of Adult Education
University of Technology, Sydney

Acknowledgements

This book could not have been compiled without the involvement and support of many people in the activities of the Learning-oriented Assessment Project (LOAP). This project, based in the Hong Kong Institute of Education, was made possible by a Teaching Development Grant awarded by the University Grants Committee for which we express our gratitude.

Firstly, we would like to thank Paul Morris, President of the Hong Kong Institute of Education (HKIEd). His inspiration and support from the beginning of the project to its conclusion has contributed greatly to the success of LOAP.

Secondly, we would like to acknowledge the sterling contributions of our four consultants: David Boud, Peter Knight, Lewis Elton and Graham Gibbs. Their visits to Hong Kong and the input they provided did much to raise the profile of the project and their advice and support were instrumental in steering us in appropriate directions. Royce Sadler visited the HKIEd towards the end of the project and also provided extremely helpful and insightful advice.

This book is one of the main outputs of the project. David Boud and Royce Sadler provided detailed comments on early versions, while Sally Brown and Phil Race suggested numerous improvements to the penultimate draft. In our work on this book, we are also indebted to our consultants in a less tangible but equally important way — their published work has had a major influence on the book's conceptual framework, and indeed on our entire thinking about learning-oriented assessment. While the style of this book avoids extensive in-text referencing, we would like to emphasize our particular indebtedness to the works of our consultants listed in the Appendix.

Thirdly, we would like to thank other LOAP team members for their contributions to the wider project: Magdalena Mok Mo-ching, Rita Chan Yin-ping, Atara Sivan, Philip Beh, Maureen Tam, Mike Keppell, Pamela Leung, Sylvia Tang Yee-fan, Hui Ming-fai, Doris Cheng, and Rita Yip Lai-chi.

We are also grateful to our research assistants and student helpers who supported the project over its three-year duration. Maggie Chan Sau-yee deserves particular mention for her long-term commitment to the project, her organizational skills and her key role in supporting the compilation of the book.

Last but not least, we would like to thank the contributors to the book. Their work forms the heart of the book in Chapter 3. Their collegial spirit in sharing their ideas plays a significant role in the further development of learning-oriented assessment practices.

1

Improving Assessment, Improving Learning

What this book is about

The genesis of this book lies in the Learning-oriented Assessment Project (LOAP) which sought to identify, promote and disseminate useful practices in assessment that would promote productive learning. The project was based in the Hong Kong Institute of Education and included all the tertiary institutions in Hong Kong.

This book is about improving student learning: there are many ways to enhance student learning and the strategy that this book promotes is through assessment. Assessment is an appropriate focus because it is one element of the instructional process that cannot be avoided since institutions require assessments for certification purposes. We seek to refigure assessment so that it not only measures or judges student achievement but also contributes to positive learning experiences. What is more, assessment also helps us to teach more effectively by identifying what students know and do not know, where confusion lies, and where we might most productively concentrate our instruction. Adjusting our assessment practices has enormous potential for improving student learning and providing us with more satisfying teaching experiences. This is the heart of this book.

Assessment and teachers

Lecturers in higher education are busy people facing multiple demands. Our academic interests are usually divided between our disciplines, our research in particular areas of it, our students and their learning. We want our students to learn well, but we are sometimes frustrated by their shortcomings. Few of us have a passion for assessment. In fact, assessment is more likely to be seen as an enemy than an ally in our work. Doing assessment well may be more arduous than recycling what has gone on before. Indeed, assessment often involves time-consuming procedures such as setting examination papers and assignments, marking them, collating scores, carrying out moderation and attending Examiners Boards. But can assessment be more than this? Can assessment become a satisfying part of teaching, rather than a drudge?

Assessment often engenders strong emotions. As students or lecturers, we have probably all experienced some negative experiences associated with assessment. At a basic level, many of us may simply feel a lack of enthusiasm for the endless tasks of marking assignments or exam scripts. Despite its unpopular image, we cannot escape from assessment, even though some of us may often wish we could do so. The motivation for transforming assessment and handling it more productively is therefore strong, particularly in view of the considerable dissatisfaction with aspects of current practices. This book contains many examples of how assessment can be made more humane, less unpleasant and more focused on the positive business of enhancing student learning.

Assessment and learning

We are all aware of the influence assessment has on the teaching and learning process. It affects all students and all lecturers in ways that may be positive, benign or negative. Assessment impacts on what content students focus on, their approaches to learning, and their patterns of study. What they do for their assignments and their preparation for examinations, and how they perceive the results of this assessment, have a profound impact on them both as learners and as individuals. Students follow the cues we give them via assessment and this helps them make choices about how they spend their time, so our assessment design needs to be undertaken carefully to maximize the positive impact of assessment on student behaviour. In short, assessment has such power that it is essential that we handle it so that its learning potential is fully harnessed.

Assessment and the curriculum

Knowledge is generally accepted as being realized through three components which interlock and interact. These components are curriculum, pedagogy and assessment. Assessment has a powerful impact on the curriculum; in fact, from the student perspective it often defines the curriculum (Ramsden, 2003). In other words, the assessment components of the curriculum are often more influential than what is written in formal course documentation. Following from this, a common way of instigating curriculum reform is through changing assessment. The term 'backwash' represents this impact that assessment reform has on teaching and learning. Engendering positive backwash can be stimulated through integrating sound assessment within curriculum processes rather than it being something that occurs at its end. Biggs (2003) extends this through the notion of constructive alignment, integrating constructivist teaching methods, learning objectives phrased as outcomes, module content and assessment methods. He holds that student learning is most effective when we align learning outcomes, how we teach and how we assess.

Assessment and outcomes

Outcomes-based education means focusing efforts on student achievement of clearly defined outcomes we want all students to achieve. Biggs's concept of constructive alignment depends on a clear understanding of what it is that students need to achieve, that is, of the learning outcomes for their particular modules and programmes. Outcomes-based education has become a prominent theme for Hong Kong universities, as it is in many parts of the world, so it is an important factor in our consideration of learning and assessment. Learning outcomes operate at various levels, each of which has implications for assessment.

One specific level involves learning outcomes expressed in terms of subject-specific performance in a module or unit. These criteria become important guide posts for student learning. They become the point of reference for teachers' feedback on students' work, and are an essential tool in helping students to develop their self-evaluation capacities as they learn to compare their work against these criteria.

A second broader level involves learning outcomes as expressions of overarching abilities that an overall programme is seeking to develop in its students (see, for example, Maki, 2004). This involves students in becoming not only proficient in subject-specific knowledge, but also developing more generic abilities such as problem-solving, communication skills, the capacity to work well with others, and the ability to continue learning in whatever work contexts they will eventually find themselves. It is no coincidence that all of the assessment practices presented in Chapter 3 of this book work to develop these kinds of skills in students.

The challenges of assessment

What are the main challenges related to assessment which this book seeks to tackle? We identify some of the main challenges as follows: the multiple demands of assessment; an examination-oriented system which often leads to surface learning; issues of grade distribution and standards; providing effective feedback to large classes; managing the logistics of group assessments; and plagiarism. These are discussed below as a starting-point for the book and we return to these issues with some recommended strategies in Chapter 4.

Double duty in assessment

A fundamental challenge is that assessment is about several things at once (Ramsden, 2003). It is about learning and it is about grading; it is about summarizing student achievements and about teaching them better; it is about standards and invoking comparisons between individuals; it concerns what students can do now and what they might do in the future; it has technical aspects and social ones; it communicates explicit and hidden messages. Assessment engenders tensions and compromises. Boud (2000) uses the term 'double duty' to represent the dualities of assessment and provides three examples: assessments have to encompass formative assessment for learning and summative assessment for certification; they have to focus on the immediate task and equipping students for lifelong learning; and they have to attend to the learning process and the substantive content domain. Recommending shifts in assessment practice is particularly hampered by this realization that assessments do double duty. The complexity of assessment and its multiple demands makes reform difficult to achieve, but essential to educational progress.

Examinations distorting learning

Assessment can distort the learning process. For example, it can lead to some important topics being neglected by students, whilst others are afforded undue importance. It may mean that certain skills are overemphasized, such as the memorization and regurgitation of information, whilst other skills are neglected. There is a danger that examinations assess lower-order outcomes which are easily assessable, whilst higher-order outcomes are neglected. For example, it is increasingly being recognized that the workforce of the twenty-first century requires generic skills such as communication, problem-solving, collaboration, and critical thinking. Examinations rarely encourage the development of these skills. They may be superficially attractive in terms of providing an apparently level playing-field and avoiding the scourge of Internet plagiarism, but they may not encourage deep understanding, and they may leave students with a satisfactory mark but little else to show for their effort. Biggs argues that inappropriate testing can have a negative impact on student learning and that "low level, surface approaches to learning exist not because of an intrinsic defect in the student but because of a teaching and testing context that encourages such behaviour and allows it to work" (Biggs, 1996: 298).

Examinations make thoughtful planning, drafting, redrafting and self-evaluation for improvement difficult, so students are unlikely to produce their best performance under test conditions. A further disadvantage is that unless an end of course examination is combined with other methods, it can make it harder to identify student difficulties until it is too late. Following from these points, a key theme of the book is the setting of assessment tasks that stimulate the kind of learning we want students to engage in, and that lead to the outcomes we want them to achieve.

The bell curve

Norm-referenced assessment compares students with each other, with students' results typically being distributed according to a 'normal' or bell-shaped curve. Explicit or implicit pressure to comply with fixed mark distributions of this kind can represent an unwanted side-effect of grading student work. Although it seems that in recent years fewer universities explicitly demand a bell curve of grades, there is often an implicit expectation that there will be a spread of grades and not too many grades at the top.

Criterion-referenced assessment, in contrast, considers what students have learnt in relation to intended outcomes expressed as performance criteria. These criteria provide a basis for students to judge their ongoing progress.

The residual impact of norm-referenced assessment can, however, cast a cloud over criterion-referenced assessment. One way for tutors to apply criteria is on the basis of comparisons with other students and whilst tutors accept that students should be judged according to the criteria, they may still tend to believe that a rigorous assessment should provide a spread of marks — this may or may not be the case. Whilst concerns about declining standards or grade inflation may have some justification (Johnson, 2003), distributing grades according to a pre-set curve makes assessment a competition rather than a quest for high standards. Comparing students with each other rather than with an explicit standard is an attack on standards rather than a defence of them because however good the teaching, however good the student performance, some students are destined to be awarded relatively low grades. Good teaching and good learning should lead to a large number of students achieving high grades. We need to be prepared to argue this point during Boards of Examiners meetings and provide evidence, where necessary, to support our assertions.

Modularization

Modular systems of higher education may exacerbate assessment and learning problems. The main challenge, from the student viewpoint, is often having the same or similar assessment deadlines for assessment in different modules. A series of assessment deadlines are likely to accumulate towards the end of a semester. This tends to discourage students from spreading their learning effort evenly throughout the term. It may also mean that students are unable to produce their best performance simply because they become overloaded.

Students may also find it difficult to make connections between modules. From the student viewpoint, coherence may not be evident so a student may find it difficult to use learning from one module on an assessment task for another module. From the lecturers' perspective, it may increase workloads if more than one assessment task is included within a short modular timeframe. The modular system may also distance the student from her lecturers as she moves from tutor to tutor in quick succession and her learning problems may not be addressed or followed up. It may also be difficult for the student to utilize feedback from one module in another.

Feedback and marking loads

A further challenge is providing effective feedback within the constraints of large class sizes and associated heavy marking loads. Academics may find that they are spending inordinate amounts of time engaged in marking activities, but may ponder the extent to which they are using their time productively. Feedback is central to the learning process and when handled effectively it can be one of the most powerful ways of enhancing student learning. However, the way assessment is currently handled results in students often receiving feedback several weeks after a module is completed. This relates to a problem identified internationally (Higgins, Hartley and Skelton, 2001, 2002) and reinforced by our work (Carless, 2006; Liu, 2005), that much feedback in higher education comes too late for students to be able to make significant use of it. Feedback is labour-intensive for tutors to provide, so it is particularly unfortunate if it is not carried out efficiently and becomes a cause of frustration for both tutors and students. Large class sizes and the way assessment is currently handled reduce the potential for tutor feedback and increase the challenge of providing helpful feedback to students in user-friendly ways.

Group assignments

A useful strategy in assessing large classes is group projects or group assignments. This has an academic rationale in terms of encouraging skills such as planning, negotiation, compromise and team-work. In other words, it encourages the kind of skills that are essential in the workplace, while also engendering peer learning. There is also a pragmatic rationale — group assignments can substantially reduce lecturers' marking loads. The main problems of group assignments relate to the difficulty of allocating fair individual grades to group members. A further challenge is that much useful peer learning may take place, but that this process of learning may not be easily identifiable from final assessment products.

Plagiarism

Plagiarism is a long-standing assessment problem but one that seems to have been exacerbated by modern technologies (Carroll, 2005). The Internet is a wonderful source of information but is also open to misuse. How can tutors be confident that what they are reading are the efforts of the student rather than something that has been cut and pasted from the Internet? It is generally agreed that plagiarism thrives in large classes because plagiarism thrives on anonymity. Examinations are one possible solution to plagiarism, but they substitute one problem with another one as discussed above.

The aim and structure of this book

How will you benefit from reading this book? We hope that considering the range of practices described in this book, reflecting on them, and adopting or adapting them in your own context, will help your students to learn better and so provide you with more satisfying teaching experiences, as well as making your assessment practices more manageable. The book is designed to provide some new perspectives on the assessment process and its relationship to student learning. It provides an insight into current state-of-the-art instructional practices in tertiary institutions in Hong Kong and as such it can broaden your repertoire of techniques.

This book contains assessment techniques which tackle the challenges outlined above. It provides a source of good practices, tried and tested in the Hong Kong context, which are designed with student learning foremost in mind. But it does more than this. It locates these practices within a framework for assessment based on some of the best research and scholarship available in this field.

The remainder of the book is organized as follows. Chapter 2 presents a conceptual framework for assessment. It summarizes some of the key concepts associated with assessment in the service of learning and develops the theoretical bases for the collection of practices which follow. The framework highlights three key concepts which underpin the collection: assessment tasks as learning tasks; student involvement in assessment; and the notion of feedback as 'feedforward'.

Chapter 3 presents thirty-nine separate assessment techniques, selected following a series of reviews of the sixty-four techniques submitted for consideration. Each technique is set out in a structured way to allow easy reading, and includes procedures, student comments, and suggestions for how the technique can be used in different contexts. Each technique has been chosen because it clearly supports student learning and can be adapted by other academics in a range of disciplines and teaching contexts.

Chapter 4 draws out some of the wider implications of the framework and the practices and examines some of the progress which has been made within the theme of assessment change. It examines some inhibiting factors impeding the rejuvenation of assessment processes and suggests some strategies for tackling these challenges.

The Appendix provides an annotated bibliography of articles, web sites and other sourcebooks that we have found to be most useful. We hope that these can inform the interested reader's further investigations into the interface between teaching, learning and assessment.

2

A Conceptual Framework for Learning-oriented Assessment

This book presents different techniques used by teachers across a range of disciplines in higher education. Each technique is concerned with assessment in some form. Each one is also designed to improve students' learning.

These techniques are more than simply good ideas. While they are valuable because they have demonstrated their worth in practice, how they contribute to learning fits within a framework for learning-oriented assessment that encompasses some of the best thinking and research on assessment and learning in higher education. This chapter describes the framework which helps to illuminate the practices presented in Chapter 3. Each of these practices is underpinned by some aspects of the framework.

'Learning-oriented assessment'

We have coined the term 'learning-oriented assessment' (Carless, Joughin and Mok, 2006) to describe an approach to assessment which seeks to bring to the foreground those aspects of assessment that encourage or support students' learning. While we are used to thinking of assessment in terms of judgements about students' achievements, 'learning-oriented assessment' seeks to balance this understanding by drawing our attention to the crucial role that assessment can play in promoting productive student learning. Learning-oriented assessment is assessment designed to support learning — regardless of any other functions it may be performing, learning-oriented assessment is planned and implemented with the development of learning firmly in mind. Our conceptualization of learning-oriented assessment is developed further below.

Promoting learning, along with judging students' achievements and maintaining the standards of a profession or discipline are three core functions of assessment. A well planned assessment regime performs all three functions, holding them in balance and integrating them so that they substantially (and ideally totally) overlap. Figure 2.1 below illustrates these three functions.

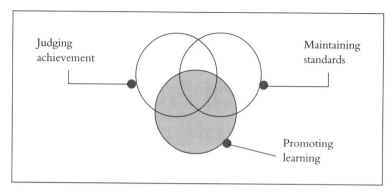

Figure 2.1   The main purposes of assessment

Learning-oriented assessment, summative assessment and formative assessment

The terms 'summative' and 'formative' are commonly used to describe assessment when it is used for the purposes of judging achievement and promoting ongoing learning respectively. They are noted here because learning-oriented assessment encompasses both of these assessment functions. We saw in Chapter 1 that summmative assessment can distort the learning process if it leads students to ignore important topics and to focus on lower-order outcomes. However, summative assessment can equally have a positive influence on what students focus on in their study and how they learn as they prepare for and undertake assessment for grades. When summative assessment is learning-oriented, that is, when it is designed with learning, as well as judging, in mind, it can direct students to concentrate on developing their understanding of important content while cultivating key intellectual and generic skills. As we noted in Chapter 1, when summative assessment is aligned with such learning outcomes, deep rather than surface learning is more likely to occur.

Formative assessment is always learning-oriented since its purpose is to identify students' strengths and areas for improvement in order to shape their ongoing learning. The term 'learning-oriented assessment' highlights the need for such assessment. While formative assessment can take many forms, both formal and informal, one of the greatest challenges in higher education is to design *summative* assessment so that it performs a formative function.

The elements of learning-oriented assessment

While the design of summative and formative assessment tasks are central to learning, learning-oriented assessment builds on and extends these notions (Joughin, 2005) so that for us, learning-oriented assessment is concerned with three things:

- designing assessment tasks that engage students in processes that lead to learning — what we term 'assessment tasks as learning tasks';
- involving students in the process of evaluating their own work and that of their peers, a skill that is an important part of effective learning, as well as being crucial in their later professional lives; and

- building complete feedback loops into learning so that students act on information received — the key concept here is 'feedforward', as students use information provided to progress their work and their learning.

While these three elements are at the heart of learning-oriented assessment, their ultimate value lies in how they lead to desired learning outcomes. Learning-oriented assessment focuses on the quality of student learning outcomes through applying the above three processes to help students achieve key disciplinary and generic understanding, values and skills.

Figure 2.2 sets out these elements of learning-oriented assessment in graphic form.

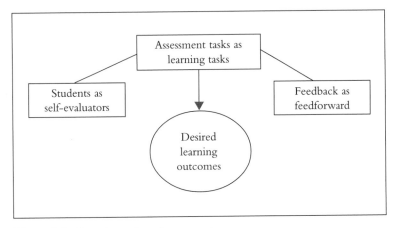

Figure 2.2   Learning-oriented assessment

From the understanding of learning-oriented assessment outlined above, we can see that the key question in considering any particular assessment practice is "How does this assessment practice support learning?" We believe that an important part of the answer to this lies in the three elements of learning-oriented assessment which we will unpack in more detail in the following sections.

Assessment tasks as learning tasks

We noted in Chapter 1 the powerful influence that assessment requirements have on students' learning. Consequently, an effective way to channel student learning is by adjusting the tasks they are required to do, and the way they are encouraged to carry them out, so that these become prime ways of learning. In other words, assessment tasks are constructed so that they become learning tasks as well. 'Assessment tasks as learning tasks' is therefore the overarching element of our framework for learning-oriented assessment.

'Assessment tasks as learning tasks' work most powerfully when the process involved in completing the assessment task is actually the same as the learning process. An assignment that requires students to engage in a process of inquiry (see practice 4 in Chapter 3), a project that can only be completed by research, peer discussion and the application of theory to practice (see practice 2, Chapter 3), or an essay that requires independent research and structured interaction with the lecturer (see practice 1, Chapter 3) are examples of learning processes that culminate in an assessed product. This close alignment of assessment tasks with learning activities is at the heart of Biggs's 'constructive alignment' noted in Chapter 1.

Designing assessment tasks as learning tasks is far from straightforward, for as we have seen in Chapter 1, some assessment tasks (for example, examinations) can fail to generate the kind of skills that are the espoused objectives of our courses. However, there are some points that we can usefully keep in mind in order to develop effective assessment tasks which engage students in learning activities and lead to high quality outcomes. These tasks are likely to have some, and possibly all, of the following characteristics:

- They are often closely related to some kind of 'real-life' activity, reflecting what students will need to do in their chosen field of practice.
- They are likely to provide some particular challenge and interest to students.
- They clearly and directly promote the knowledge and skills that the course requires, so students appreciate the purpose and value of the tasks.
- The tasks extend, rather than duplicate, what is done in class time.

Gibbs and Simpson have provided a good summary of how such assessment tasks support learning. They describe how assessment can be used to ensure that students do enough work, that this work is spread across the semester, and that it promotes good learning. They specify four conditions under which assessment tasks function as learning tasks:

> - Assessed tasks capture sufficient time and effort.
> - These tasks distribute student effort evenly across topics and weeks.
> - These tasks engage students in productive learning activity.
> - Assessment communicates clear and high expectations to students.
>
> (Gibbs and Simpson, 2004)

Students as evaluators of their own work

Once students are engaged in assessment tasks that promote their learning, the second element of our framework involves them in developing the capacity to evaluate the work they are doing as they complete these tasks. This capacity is important for two reasons: it is essential if students are to become independent learners who can monitor and improve the quality of their work while they are engaged in formal study, and, just as importantly, they need this capacity if they are to become lifelong learners and effective professional practitioners in the workplace.

Assessment processes are often something of a mystery to students, particularly when the assessment is always done by tutors, and when students have no real understanding of the criteria which are being used. Students can have many unanswered questions: What is the tutor looking for? What is good performance? What do I need to do to get a high mark? How do I know if I have met the required standards?

By involving students in the assessment process, students can take important steps in coming to grips with criteria and standards in their chosen field, learning what constitutes good work, and developing the capacity to evaluate the quality of their own work. Peer assessment and self-assessment are two of the best known and most useful practices for allowing this to happen. These practices become particularly powerful when students can compare their peers' assessment of their work to their own self-assessment of the work.

Assessment usually involves two kinds of activities. Firstly, it involves getting information about a person's knowledge, understanding, attitudes or skills. We usually do this by looking at their work, observing how they do certain things, or talking with them. Secondly, it involves having a sense of what that work should be like — what its different elements are and how well they should be done, or what we often term 'criteria' and 'standards'. Then we look at the gap between performance and standards, make judgements about the quality of the student's work, and suggest ways to improve it.

Involving students in assessment means engaging them in these processes, helping them to look at their own and others' work in a thoughtful and informed way, with a view to improving it. Sadler (1989), in his seminal article, described this process in terms of how students become evaluators of their own work through developing a sense of the standard of work they should be aiming for; comparing their level of performance with this standard; and taking action to close the gap between the standard and their own performance.

Involving student in their assessment in these ways has several benefits: it helps students to come to grips with the nature of good work in their discipline as they consider criteria and standards and apply these to work of varying quality; it helps students to develop the ability to evaluate their own work, something that will be crucial in their working lives; it helps students to understand how their work is assessed by tutors, letting them know more about how assessors' minds work, and what the assessment criteria actually mean in practice; in large classes or when a tutor's time is limited, it can provide an opportunity for students to receive a greater amount of timely feedback that can help them to review and revise their work; and it helps to develop a collaborative approach to learning.

The heart of self and peer assessment is not marking or grading, though sometimes this may be part of the process. The important thing is that students are actively reviewing their own work, providing feedback on their peers' work, and receiving and responding to feedback from others.

Self-assessment is often combined with peer assessment; many of the same processes and skills apply to both. Peer assessment is perhaps more common because it is a social activity which takes advantage of students' natural propensity to engage with their peers and the readily available opportunity to give and receive feedback to and from their peers. Self-assessment, by its nature, is often more of a private, individual activity, but one which can be developed and facilitated through classroom activities. In peer assessment, peer contributions may take the form of questions, comments or challenges. With self-assessment, it is the learners who are empowered to make a judgement about the value of the various inputs they have received and the direction they might take. As Boud (1995) has pointed out in another influential work on self-assessment, this process goes beyond strategies and techniques; it is a transformative process that changes how students see themselves and their learning.

Both self and peer assessment make important contributions to lifelong learning and lead us to propose another condition under which assessment supports learning:

> • Students' involvement in assessment helps them develop the capacity to evaluate their own work.

Students' capacity to evaluate their own work has another particularly important benefit in terms of our framework for learning-oriented assessment: it enables students to make sense of feedback provided by tutors or peers and to act on this feedback as they seek to improve their work. This leads us to the third element of our framework.

Feedback as feedforward

We noted in Chapter 1 that feedback is essential for student learning but that it is time-consuming to provide and is often received too late to be of maximum benefit to students. We emphasized that it needs to be forward-looking so that that it can improve students' learning and enhance their future performance on assessed tasks.

Feedback performs many important functions. It helps clarify what good performance is; it encourages teacher and peer dialogue; it supports self-assessment; it gives students quality information about their learning; it encourages self-esteem; and it provides opportunities for students to bridge the gap between current and desired performance (Nicol and Macfarlane-Dick, 2006).

How feedback works to improve students' learning seems to involve three main factors:
- Firstly, there needs to be an *appreciation* of the student's work, recognizing what has been achieved and where further development is required.
- Secondly, there needs to be an *explanation* of this appraisal, by relating feedback to the purpose of the work and to the criteria used in judging its quality. This explanation needs to be made in a way that can be understood by the student and that will encourage the student to pay careful attention to it. Opportunities for clarification, dialogue and ongoing discussion are often required for students to learn from the feedback provided.
- Thirdly and most importantly, there should be opportunity for *action* by the student based on what he or she has learnt from the feedback. This may be in a revised piece of work, or in the next assignment, but if it is the latter, the next assignment needs to follow reasonably promptly. It is probably beyond the capacity of most students if feedback needs to be acted upon several months after it has been received. This leads to a further principle that feedback should be *timely*; it needs to be received at a time that is useful to students and when they can act upon it to 'feedforward' to future work.

Feedback is typically provided by tutors, but students themselves are often effective providers of timely feedback that can be acted upon as outlined above. Some students provide insightful feedback, others less so. Student feedback may gain in promptness what it may lose in sophistication.

Gibbs and Simpson provide very helpful guidance in noting the conditions that need to apply if feedback is to function effectively to support student learning. These conditions provide an illuminating backdrop to many of the practices presented in Chapter 3.

Quantity and timing of feedback
- Sufficient feedback is provided often enough and in enough detail.
- The feedback is provided quickly enough to be useful to students.

Quality of feedback
- Feedback focuses on learning rather than on marks or students.
- Feedback is linked to the purpose of the assignment and to criteria.
- Feedback is understandable to students, given their sophistication.

Student response to feedback
- Feedback is received by students and attended to.
- Feedback is acted upon by students to improve their work or their learning.

(Gibbs and Simpson, 2004)

Learning-oriented assessment and learning outcomes

The three elements of learning-oriented assessment that we have considered so far — the design of assessment tasks as learning tasks, the development of students' self-evaluation capacities, and the use of feedback as an influential learning device — are powerful mechanisms for learning. However, they are not concepts that should be used for their own sake. They are important only when they are used to help students achieve the required learning outcomes of their particular courses, units and programmes.

We noted in Chapter 1 that important learning outcomes are likely to include both generic capabilities such as problem-solving and teamwork, and more specific outcomes related to a particular discipline or subject. Learning-oriented assessment is concerned with both levels of outcome. Discipline-specific outcomes need to be considered in the context of each discipline. On the other hand, generic outcomes are becoming increasingly important in higher education and are well supported by the assessment practices outlined in Chapter 3. Indeed, these outcomes provide the most appropriate framework for organizing the practices in that chapter.

A consolidated framework for learning-oriented assessment

By amalgamating Figures 2.1 and 2.2 we now arrive at our framework for learning-oriented assessment (Figure 2.3). From the three main purposes of assessment, we have highlighted the learning purpose as being central to our aim of improving student learning. We have discussed the three core components of a learning-oriented approach to assessment and noted the central role of learning outcomes.

Mindful that learning-oriented assessment is far from being just a technical matter, we have included on the left and right hand sides the important student and staff perspectives on and experiences of assessment. Based on their previous experience and their beliefs about assessment,

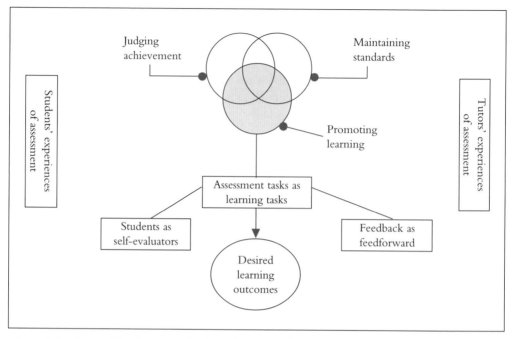

Figure 2.3   A consolidated framework of learning-oriented assessment

learning and teaching, tutors and students can understand and respond to assessment in a variety of contrasting ways. For example, students whose experience of assessment has been limited to traditional methods may be reluctant to accept innovative assessment methods. Tutors will need to explain and justify the rationale for a chosen strategy so that students can see how they will benefit from it. Tutors' capacity to be innovative is often constrained by their own limited experience of assessment formats. A core purpose of this book is to provide tutors with a variety of alternative assessment methods that can be adapted or customized for their context. Learning-oriented assessment therefore needs to take into account how students and tutors alike experience assessment and help them develop their capacity to use assessment in new ways to promote learning. There is clearly much scope for greater collaboration between staff in sharing their assessment practices and for enhancing the opportunities for staff to expand their repertoire of assessment practices through professional development activities.

    We believe that this framework provides a useful conceptualization of how assessment can serve learning better. How it is implemented in practice is illustrated by the techniques in Chapter 3. Many of these techniques support learning in several ways and each is useful in promoting particular generic outcomes. Each technique also highlights aspects of the learning-oriented assessment framework. Some particularly emphasize the nature of the assessment task as learning task, with the assessment task carefully constructed in order to give structure and direction to students' learning activities. Some explicitly involve students in evaluating their own work and/ or that of their peers. Others pay special attention to feedback processes by ensuring feedback is timely, helpful and acted on. Of course, these aspects are not mutually exclusive and many practices exhibit more than one of them. However, each practice does tend to highlight one aspect. For readers who may wish to explore a particular aspect of learning-oriented assessment, Table 2.1 draws attention to elements of learning-oriented assessment that are highlighted in each practice found in Chapter 3.

Table 2.1 How specific assessment practices support learning

Assessment tasks as learning tasks	Students as self-evaluators	Feedback as feedforward
1, 2, 3, 4, 10, 14, 18, 19, 26, 27, 31	11, 15, 20, 21, 22, 23, 24, 25, 32, 33, 34	5, 6, 7, 8, 9, 12, 13, 16, 17, 28, 29, 30, 35, 36, 37, 38, 39

Summary

This chapter has presented our conception of learning-oriented assessment. We view assessment as supporting learning when tasks are focused on sound learning, when students are involved in the assessment process in ways which promote their own self-monitoring ability, when feedback is forward-looking, and when all of these factors are moving students towards the achievement of worthwhile learning outcomes. In this way, the assessment practices in Chapter 3 are supported by a framework of general principles. These principles can be used to generate and validate new techniques congruent with the framework.

3
Assessment Practices That Promote Learning

This chapter presents 39 specific assessment practices from academics teaching in a range of Hong Kong higher education institutions. These practices share a number of qualities which we believe make them useful for academics in many contexts:

- Each one is an actual practice, used by real academics with real students. The practices are not theories or simply good ideas, though they may be based on a theoretical understanding of learning and are certainly the result of careful thought by their contributors.
- Each practice has been shown to work well in the context in which it was developed.
- Each practice has been valued by students, though their evaluative comments have not always been uncritical.
- Each practice has a wide application. We believe each can be applied to a range of disciplines.
- Each is adaptable and lends itself to modification to suit particular contexts.
- Most importantly, each supports student learning and contributes to important learning outcomes.
- Each practice relates to our theoretical framework in Chapter 2.

The practices are not considered to be 'perfect'; of course, there is no such thing in education. Neither can they be simply applied to a new situation without modification. They are presented in the hope that they will stimulate thought, be adapted in small or major ways, and lead to better, more satisfying practice for teachers and better learning experiences for students.

Generic learning outcomes

In Chapters 1 and 2 we noted the growing importance of learning outcomes as a key way of thinking about teaching, learning and assessment in higher education. We pointed out that the value of the learning-oriented assessment practices included in this book lies not only in how they support student learning processes, but how these processes in turn lead to desired learning outcomes. We also noted that learning outcomes can be defined at different levels, and that an important way of considering learning outcomes is as expressions of overarching capabilities that an overall programme is seeking to develop in its students. While the practices described in this chapter focus on assessment and learning, each one makes an important contribution to students' development of one or more such capabilities. It is therefore appropriate for the practices to be considered in the light of how they contribute to these.

Much has been written about the desirability of making these capabilities explicit and integrating them in undergraduate learning. Most universities have developed, or are developing, a list of capabilities, typically in terms of the desired attributes of their graduates. Alverno College in the United States is well known for developing its programmes around the development of eight abilities: communication, analysis, problem-solving, valuing in decision-making, social interaction, developing a global perspective, effective citizenship, and aesthetic engagement (see, for example, Mentkowski et al., 2000). In Australia, the Course Experience Questionnaire which is administered to all graduates refers to six generic skills: team work, analysis, problem-solving, written communication, tackling unfamiliar problems, and planning one's own work. In Hong Kong, most universities have developed, or are developing, descriptions of the qualities that should be possessed by their graduates, along with more specific professional or disciplinary knowledge, skills and values.

The assessment practices presented in this chapter do not cover a comprehensive list of generic learning outcomes. However, they do involve students in nine very important skills that are closely aligned with the ones noted above, while also including some that are particularly important in helping students to develop their ability to learn through assessment processes. These nine skills provide the structure for this chapter. Each one is described briefly below.

Researching

Many universities are now considering how best to link undergraduate teaching and research. One way is to involve students in research activities. The purpose of such activities is largely twofold: they require students to engage with content and ideas, and they involve students in the process of discovering things for themselves as they begin to learn how knowledge is created in a particular discipline. Research-based assessment tasks can be particularly interesting and engaging for students since they often involve students in real-life activities such as field work and designing and conducting their own projects.

Higher-order thinking

'Higher-order thinking' is an umbrella term which includes problem-solving, decision-making, critical thinking, analysis and reflection. It is how we expect graduates to think, and it is how we want our students to work when they are undertaking any but the simplest tasks. Many assessment practices in this book require students to respond to complex tasks, to solve difficult problems, to analyse critically what they are reading, and to reflect in depth on their experiences. All these processes require students to engage deeply with important ideas. Other practices require students to 'think twice', that is, to extend their original thinking by critiquing their initial responses to an assessment task, frequently in the context of feedback, and often in the context of class discussion.

Communicating using technology

All graduates, and all students, need to be able to communicate well in a variety of modes. With the explosion in the use of the Internet for business, professional and personal interactions, the capacity to express one's ideas and to communicate with others online is becoming an essential skill. The ease and speed of communication, the capacity to share information using a range of media, and the ability to create virtual teams who can work creatively and efficiently have made the Internet an indispensable part of the world of work which our students will be entering. The Internet is also an integral part of learning for almost all students and it is playing an increasingly important role in their assessment. Assessment tasks can provide highly motivating contexts for students to create individual and/or group products online, to collaborate efficiently in this process, to exchange critical and constructive feedback with peers, and to revise their work accordingly. The Internet also allows for rapid interactions between student and tutor as assessment tasks and criteria are clarified, advice is sought, drafts are submitted for feedback, and, eventually, assignments are submitted and returned.

Communicating orally or in writing

Of course, more traditional forms of communication are just as important as emerging forms, so that graduates need to be able to write in a range of formats and express themselves orally. Traditional forms of assessment such as essays are valuable, while alternative forms of assessment such as reports, portfolios, case studies, and research projects develop students' ability to write in a range of useful formats. Much of our working lives depend on our ability to communicate ideas verbally, so spoken presentations and other forms of oral assessment can be particularly useful in preparing students for their future work. Moreover, many of the processes surrounding assessment tasks can promote oral communication skills. These include the teamwork involved in group assessment tasks (which is discussed below) and the discussion of feedback, whether between peers or between student and tutor.

Working in teams

Group assessment tasks introduce considerable complexity into assessment, require careful thought in their design and considerable skill on the part of the tutor in their implementation. However, they can be an excellent tool for developing students' knowledge of how teams function and their skills in working effectively with others. These include knowledge of how groups form and develop, methods for sharing work, and skills in conducting team meetings, resolving problems, and reporting results. Working in teams also allows for peer learning, as students learn with and from each other (Boud, Cohen and Sampson, 2001).

Evaluating peers

Peer evaluation involves making judgements about a fellow student's work. This may or may not include awarding a mark. What it does require is for the student evaluator to understand what makes for a good piece of work, that is, for the student to be familiar with the criteria and standards that can be applied in the evaluation process. These become the basis for comments and/or discussion with the student whose work is being evaluated. For the student evaluating, the benefits include becoming more familiar with the standards that apply in a subject, seeing how another student has tackled a task, thereby learning something from their approach, and learning through articulating their ideas about the subject when they provide feedback.

Learning autonomously

The need for us all to be 'lifelong learners' has become a catchphrase at all levels of education. At the heart of this is the process of learning autonomously, either individually or in conjunction with those around us. The rapid development of new knowledge and practices means that graduates who prosper will be those who can keep on learning after graduation as they respond to new demands, face previously unknown problems, and maintain an up-to-date awareness of developments in their field. Learning autonomously in the workplace needs to begin with learning autonomously in the university as students learn to set their own objectives, seek resources, monitor their progress, and accept responsibility for their own learning.

Evaluating oneself

"Self assessment involves students taking responsibility for monitoring and making judgements about aspects of their own learning" (Boud, 1991: 1). Like the process of evaluating peers, marks are not necessarily part of this process. What matters is that students are coming to grips with criteria and standards in their subject, learning to look at their own work critically on the basis of these criteria and standards, accepting responsibility for judging their work, and, most importantly, learning to improve their work while they are producing it. The need for students to develop the ability to evaluate themselves should be clear; in their future working lives, they will need to ensure that their work meets the standards required by their profession, their employers, or their clients.

Processing and acting on feedback

While it is vitally important for tutors to provide high quality feedback in a timely way, it is equally important that students learn to engage with this feedback, make sense of it, and act on it to improve their learning and their work. These are abilities that can and must be learnt, and assessment provides the ideal context for developing this capacity.

Of course, these nine categories are not mutually exclusive. For example, learning autonomously involves being able to evaluate one's own progress, working in teams requires the ability to communicate well and to listen to, and act on, feedback from other team members, and most of the abilities are related in some way to developing higher-order thinking skills. Because of this, any of the practices described in this chapter are likely to involve more than one of these skills. However, each practice does tend to highlight one of them, so that we have been able to use these nine skills to categorize the thirty-nine different assessment practices presented in this chapter. A few of the practices could have been equally well placed in more than one category. When this was the case, we have made a judgement and allocated the practice to one category.

The structure of each practice

Each practice is presented using a structured format for ease of reading and quick access to the practice's main features. This format includes a short summary, the background and rationale for the practice. The essence of the practice is presented under the heading of 'procedure'. Successful outcomes are noted, and in most instances, students' responses are captured in direct quotations. Many practices include supporting materials such as worksheets.

Commentary has been added at three points for each practice:

☐ We have suggested 'situations where this practice could be used' to draw the reader's attention to the many contexts in which the practice might be applied. While most practices have been developed in a specific context, all of them have wide applicability.

☐ We also include the section on 'how this practice supports learning'. Here we draw on some of the concepts underpinning learning and assessment noted in Chapter 2 and make explicit how these support the practice described by the contributor.

☐ Under the heading 'further suggestions', we suggest alternative ways in which the practice might be carried out. The purpose of this section is to support the reader in adapting the practice to his or her own context.

Adapting the practices to your context

Most importantly, the practices need to be read with an open mind. We invite you to seek out what might be useful and adapt these to your own situation. Few educational practices can be simply taken from one context to another — how you use them depends on your own thoughts about teaching, learning and assessment, the nature of your discipline and programmes, the kinds of students you teach, your institution's policies, and no doubt many other factors. We hope that you will find, amongst the range of practices in this chapter, a number of ideas that will encourage you to rethink your current assessment practices and that will lead to increased satisfaction for you as a teacher and better learning for your students.

▌ **Researching** ▌

1. Research paper assignments that prevent plagiarism

Deirdre Mary SMYTHE, St. Mary's University

Summary
Students develop research papers progressively through a proposal, first draft and final draft. Substantial, timely feedback is given on the first draft, but no marks are assigned. Students base the final draft on these comments. The final draft is marked, but no other feedback is provided.

Situations where this practice could be used
This practice could be applied to any research paper in any discipline.

Background   This technique was developed after a serious incident of plagiarism in a Chinese classroom, where fifty students in a class of one hundred senior English majors plagiarized an assignment on Toni Morisson's *The Bluest Eye* from the Internet. Extensive consideration on how to prevent plagiarism led to the development of the method.

Rationale
- ☐ Plagiarism has become a severe problem globally in higher education because of the increase in student use of the Internet. It has become easy for students to sit in front of a computer and 'cut and paste' a paper for submission, rather than taking the trouble to do traditional library research from journal articles and books.
- ☐ The practice described here creates a 'feedback loop' where students act on assessment information provided. Not only does this approach prevent plagiarism, it creates a situation where students learn from mistakes within the context of one assignment. This method works on the argument that a student is more likely to plagiarize if work is left to the last minute, and the student is under great pressure to complete a paper.

Procedure
1. Students make a decision on the research topic of their choice. The rationale for this is that students perform better if they are working on a topic of interest. They are required to submit a specific number of references, and the use of Internet web sites in their reference lists is restricted. Students are encouraged to learn how to use a library to find books, and to negotiate databases for finding scholarly articles.

2. Research paper assignments are divided into three components: a proposal, a first draft and a 'penultimate' draft. The term 'penultimate' is used here in the sense of the 'unfinished' or 'unpublished' quality of most student work, hence the use of a term meaning 'next to last' draft.

3. The proposal component becomes due within the first two weeks of classes. It forces students to begin thinking about an assignment immediately, and to make a commitment to a research topic. The proposal consists of a one-page outline of the intended research topic.

4. The first draft becomes due several weeks later — perhaps in the middle of the term. Here, all that is required is that the students make a beginning. There are no specific rules, only that a first draft is handed in for assessment.

5. No grade is assigned to the first draft, but substantial feedback or comments are provided to assist the student in completing the final draft. This component is labour-intensive, but worth it. This is given back to students fairly quickly, so that they have time to incorporate the feedback into the penultimate draft.

6. Students hand in a penultimate draft based on the comments on their first draft. Here, no comments are provided, and a grade is assigned. Guidelines for assigning a mark are the presence of a recognizable argument, strong supporting evidence and analysis, as well as proper spelling, grammar and sentence structure.

Supporting materials	None.
Outcomes worth noting	☐ This procedure is seen to reduce plagiarism in assignments significantly. It also reduces the pressure on students to perform at the last minute. The method has been successfully used in both Chinese and North American university classrooms. One of the limitations of this type of assessment is that is it is only manageable in classes of under 100, and is impossible to administer in large introductory courses with several hundred students. It also requires the support of teaching assistants for larger classes.
Student response	☐ Students appreciate the fact that they are given concrete guidance in the process of conducting their research and writing their research papers. They have reported that the method helps them to think of a research topic at the beginning of the term, and even if it is not started immediately, there is a specific direction in mind for their future work. First-year students find the notion of a proposal a little daunting, as it is unfamiliar territory. In addition, students feel pressured to 'perform' on the first draft, even though they are not being marked, and there

Researching

are usually a lot of questions around what is specifically required for the first draft component.

How this practice supports learning	• This practice inhibits plagiarism since students are required to develop their own line of inquiry and commit to researching it early. A first draft is expected to be in a relatively unpolished form — not in the form of material that could be submitted.
	• The pattern of feedback is particularly noteworthy. Extensive feedback is given when it can be of most use, with most of this feedback serving the 'feedforward' role, i.e. directly helping students to undertake the next stage of their writing.

Further suggestions	• Feedback is often most useful when students can relate it to explicit criteria and standards. The provision and discussion of criteria and standards at the proposal stage will help lead to good quality proposals. Students could be encouraged to keep them in mind as they develop the first draft, and to use them as a checklist prior to submitting the penultimate draft.
	• Students could be required to submit a self-assessment of their penultimate draft at the point of handing it in, self-assessing their work against the criteria agreed for the task. This would help them to reflect more deeply on their work, and further limit the tendency to complete the work at the last minute. A small proportion of the marks could be allocated for the quality of the self-assessment. The self-assessment would further inhibit plagiarism, as students could only reflect realistically on their own thinking.
	• Students could be asked to submit a short action plan with their penultimate draft, outlining what changes they would expect to make in order to upgrade it towards publishable status. This would help them to reflect on which parts of the work would need improvement.

Contributor

Deirdre Mary SMYTHE
Department of Sociology and Criminology
St. Mary's University
Halifax, Nova Scotia, CANADA
Email: Deirdre.Smythe@smu.ca

Researching

2. Assessing research and writing: An integrated cycle of tasks and feedback

Paul STABLES, Hong Kong Shue Yan College

Summary
This contribution describes how formative assessment and feedback can be interleaved with research tasks and micro-assignments over a period of several weeks to create the appropriate environment for the production of well-written, informed, and analytical essays.

Situations where this practice could be used
This practice can be applied in situations where
- students are required to complete a succession of tasks;
- the tasks involve independent research; and
- the work is done in groups.

Background	☐ An English poetry course taken in Year Two of a four-year honours diploma programme in English language and literature.
	☐ This description covers a group essay project worth 20%. Over a period of six weeks students develop a 1600–2400 word essay on two specified poems.
Rationale	This practice seeks to:
	☐ assist the development of student autonomy in research and thoughtful interaction with texts;
	☐ further develop a student's critical perspective and express this in a well-written essay;
	☐ encourage peer discussion and reflection; and
	☐ encourage students to take a more process orientated approach to essay writing.
Procedure	*At the beginning*
	1. Students are randomly grouped into threes by the instructor.
	2. The instructor presents a broad outline of the design of the group essay project, its aims and objectives, and the different assessment criteria and weighting for its three component parts:
	(a) micro-assignments and research tasks (40%)
	(b) first draft of a 1600–2400 word essay (20%)
	(c) final draft of the essay (40%).
	3. The instructor distributes two poems and the first instalment of the project's instructions.

Researching

The preparatory micro-assignments and research tasks

4.   Over a period of three weeks groups complete, in and out of class, preparatory micro-assignments that require significant interaction with the poems (often examining very short pieces of text) and tasks that focus on the historical and literary context of the poems.

5.   Groups submit written work and/or make short oral presentations at regular intervals. Grades are not disclosed immediately, but before preparation work continues, formative feedback is given; for written work this is often in the form of a composite example formed from the best bits of the submissions from three or four different groups.

6.   The next instalment of the project's instructions is then distributed and the preparation/research tasks continued.

Drafting, feedback, finalising

7.   When all preparation and research tasks are completed, the group writes the first draft of their project essay.

8.   At a twenty-minute conference the instructor provides feedback, makes suggestions for improvement, and awards the draft with two grades: one substantive that counts towards the project grade, and one indicative that provides a guide as to what the draft would have received had it been a final submission.

9.   After a further period of time the group submits the final version of their essay.

Assessment, feedback and moving on

10.   A report sheet is given to each group that evaluates and grades each part of their project.

11.   Before starting their second project, students discuss the lessons they have learnt from the first.

Supporting materials	☐ Two poems linked by some common element.
	☐ A detailed project instruction sheet. This is about six pages long and is given to students in instalments. It explains the aims and objectives of the project, the submission and feedback procedures, the assessment criteria, and the preparation and research tasks. Parts of the sheet are included as an appendix to illustrate the approach being taken.
Outcomes worth noting	☐ For the most part this process results in well-written, informed, and analytical essays with good development and exemplification that interact with the texts and express the opinions of the groups.
	☐ From classroom observation in subsequent courses with the same students and through formal and informal feedback from students, it seems that all aims and objectives are fulfilled to some extent but that students remain less self-reflective about their writing than they need to be.

Researching

| **Student response** | ☐ Students have rated the course highly in formal evaluations. |
| | ☐ One student who enjoyed the project praised its 'step by step' approach, she noted that it moved from the 'simple' to the 'complicated' and felt that this laid a secure foundation for the writing of an essay. |

How this practice supports learning	• This practice requires students to work steadily over the period of the semester.
	• The briefings regarding time to spend on the preparatory tasks, and relatively tight word limits for students' findings help them to structure the balance of the effort they put into the respective tasks appropriately (see Appendix, Section 1).
	• The emphasis on feedback rather than grades at the beginning stages of the process ensures that students will consider the feedback rather than focus on the grade.
	• The provision of feedback in an intensive twenty-minute meeting places feedback at the centre of the learning process and allows for the feedback to be clarified and understood.
	• The essay planning and preparation skills students develop in this project are transferable to other subjects they may be studying.
	• Incorporating discussion of the first project before commencing the second one also encourages students to learn from the feedback available through the first one.

Further suggestions	• Students could be required to undertake a self-assessment of their preparatory assignments, and submit this along with the assignments. They could then be given additional feedback on their self-assessment, and on any substantive differences between their appraisal of their work and the tutor's view of its quality.
	• After the generic feedback on the preparatory assignments is provided, groups could use this as a basis for providing more specific feedback to another group's work. This would help students to appreciate generic feedback better, and to consider how it applies to their work.
	• At the end of the conference on the first draft, groups could be invited to specify the steps they will take in response to feedback provided. This will help to ensure that the feedback is understood and will be acted on in the final version.

Researching

Contributor
Paul STABLES
Hong Kong Shue Yan College
Email: pstables@hksyc.edu

APPENDIX

Section 1   Part C — The researched response — 40%

Use the library and the Internet! Deadline 11 February by email to pstables@hksyc.edu! Remember to keep a note of all books and web sites that you use. If you use any of this material in your essay then you will need to cite your sources in the body of your essay and list them in your bibliography!

1.   Using an encyclopaedia or standard literary guide such as *The Oxford Companion to English Literature* find out as much as you can in 30 minutes about Christopher Marlowe and then summarize the information into one or two paragraphs totalling between 50 and 150 words.

2.   Using an encyclopaedia or standard literary guide such as *The Oxford Companion to English Literature* find out as much as you can in 30 minutes about Sir Walter Ralegh and then summarize the information in one or two paragraphs totalling 50 and 150 words. (Try the alternative spelling 'Raleigh' if you have problems finding him.)

3.   In literature what do we mean by a 'pastoral poem'? (Use Abrams' *A Glossary of Literary Terms* or Harmon/Holman *A Handbook to Literature* or other standard reference work.) (Summarize an answer in between 50 and 150 words.)

4.   In literature what is the difference between 'Romanticism' and 'Realism'? (Use Abrams' *A Glossary of Literary Terms* or Harmon/Holman *A Handbook to Literature* or other standard reference work.) (Summarize an answer in between 50 and 100 words.)

5.   Using an encyclopaedia find out as much as you can about the traditional rituals and customs associated with May Morning — also known as May Day (1st May). (Again 50–150 words.)

Section 2   The First Draft — 20%

Working as a group write the first draft of the following essay:
In an essay of between 1600 and 2400 words comment upon the two poems 'The Passionate Shepherd to his Love' by Christopher Marlowe and 'The Nymph's Reply to the Shepherd' by Sir Walter Ralegh. (In the conclusion to your essay it would be a good idea to refer to another poem you have read this year that explores similar themes.)

Marks will be awarded for the overall structure of your essay: an introduction (including a **draft thesis statement**), a middle section that develops, supports, and exemplifies your thesis statement, and a conclusion. You will also get credit for the quality of your ideas. A certain roughness is expected at this stage and marks will not be deducted for incomplete paragraphs, contradictions, and grammatical errors.

You will receive feedback on your first draft during a private tutorial for your group.

Section 3   The Final Submission — 40%

Working as a group finalise your essay using the feedback given in the private tutorials.
Make the support, development, and exemplification of your final thesis statement as complete as possible and proof-read carefully for language errors. Make sure all secondary sources have been cited in the body of your essay and appear in a bibliography at the end of it.

Acknowledgement

The questions and tasks in Section 1 of this project were adapted from *Poetry* by Jill Baumgaertner (New York: Harcourt Brace Jovanovich, 1990), pp. 111–3.

Researching

3.   Assessing field-based group inquiry: Feedback and reflection

Joe Tin-yau LO, The Hong Kong Institute of Education

Summary
Continuous assessment focuses on the process in which learning tasks are designed to engage students to learn reflectively in an experiential way. It can be an effective means to maximize the utility of life-wide learning through an inquiry-based approach.

Situations where this practice could be used
This practice can be used in any discipline or module when students are required to engage in authentic, inquiry-based, and/or performance-based learning tasks. It is especially feasible in project work that will engage students in process-oriented rather than solely outcome-based learning.

Background	This technique has been used with several cohorts of students taking the module, Hong Kong Studies in a Bachelor of Education programme.
Rationale	This practice seeks to: ☐ promote experiential learning; ☐ enhance independent research and learning skills; ☐ prepare students for authentic assessment; and ☐ encourage co-operative learning through group work.
Procedure	1. Students select relevant social themes/issues for conducting field-based inquiry in groups of three. Guidelines for this inquiry process are provided. 2. Inquiry outlines and plans, together with literature reviews, have to be sent to the lecturer for preliminary review and consultation. 3. The teacher provides on-going feedback to students during the process of inquiry. This is done via face-to-face consultation, e-mail and a chat room. 4. Students who have finished their field-based inquiry projects are required to share their findings with their peers through oral presentations. 5. Evaluation and feedback are given by the lecturer and peers for improvement/revision. Assessment criteria are provided. 6. Final written group reports with self-reflections are submitted for summative assessment. 7. Reports are double-marked with detailed and constructive comments and suggestions for improvement from lecturers.

Researching

Supporting materials	□	Guidelines for group inquiry
	□	Oral presentation feedback form
	□	Current literature and research reports from various sources
	□	Multimedia resources
	□	Networking with various NGOs and other cultural or government organizations for community resources
Outcomes worth noting	□	Students' feedback shows that they could learn from multiple perspectives and that the learning tasks could deepen their understanding of local issues through case studies.
	□	Rubrics have to be carefully devised with students' participation.
	□	Process-oriented and inquiry-based learning allows more room for students' reflective practice.
Student response	□	Oral presentations conducted as preliminary reports have provided good opportunities for continuous improvement through self and peer evaluations.
	□	Students find that they can develop learning skills through social inquiry projects. They can learn more in the research process of data collection and interpretation.
	□	Students report that they have found it more interesting and intellectually stimulating to learn outside the classroom.
	□	Students who have come from science backgrounds might have difficulty in conducting social inquiry. They have required lecturers to conduct workshops for them in this particular area.
	□	Some students have experienced conflicts regarding workload distribution amongst group members. It may take time and effort to help them see the paradox of independence and interdependence in cooperative learning.
	□	Some students find this kind of 'open inquiry' time-consuming and therefore burdensome in terms of assessment load.
How this practice supports learning	•	Students select their own themes and plans for their inquiry. Students are often more motivated when they can choose areas of particular interest to them. This process also begins to get them engaged with the requirements of the course. Involvement in 'real-life' settings can be highly motivating and stimulating.
	•	A variety of feedback mechanisms are available.
	•	Making work public through oral presentations to peers often leads students to produce better quality work — they don't want to let their peers down, and also want to give a good impression of themselves.
	•	The exposure to other students' work, and the need to give feedback on this, helps students develop a sense of standards required and the

Researching

criteria that can be used to judge others' work, and hence their own work. Peer evaluation can be a window to learn from others and a mirror to reflect on oneself.

- Working in a team creates opportunities for dialogue, challenge and developing the capacity to work with others.

Further suggestions	• When students are exposed to new forms of assessment and/or learning, they often uncertain about what is expected of them. The beginning phases of inquiry-based work can be particularly challenging for many students. Opportunities for students to share experiences and discuss problems early in the process may be useful.
	• It may be useful to involve the students themselves in drafting the peer assessment criteria for their presentations, and the self-assessment criteria for their final reflective reports. This would give them a greater sense of ownership of the standards towards which they are working, and would help to clarify the goals — especially useful for those students who might find themselves outside their 'comfort zones' in this kind of collaborative inquiry.

Contributor
Joe Tin-yau LO
Department of Mathematics, Science, Social Sciences and Technology
The Hong Kong Institute of Education
Email: joelo@ied.edu.hk

Researching

4. Critical incident analysis for assessment

Jean MORRISSEY, University of Dublin

Summary

This technique, known as critical incident analysis, encourages learners to make the transition from theory to practice. It requires them to identify and reflect on an incident in which they feel their intervention really made a difference in professional practice and outcomes. It is a flexible, creative and potent assessment tool that enhances learning by developing students' reflective ability and bridging the theory-practice gap.

Situations where this practice could be used

This technique could be used in many disciplines where practitioner-client relationship or human relationship in general is the focus. These include architecture, engineering, medicine, nursing, social work and teacher education.

Background	This technique has been used with undergraduate student nurses in Hong Kong in a thirteen-week module called Human Relationships and Nursing.
Rationale	This practice seeks to ☐ integrate learning, feedback and assessment; ☐ enhance students' research skills and reflective ability; and ☐ bridge the gap between theory and practice.
Procedure	1. Using Benner's (1984) guidelines, students are introduced to critical incident analysis to help them understand what constitutes a 'critical incident'. Students are required to identify a critical incident concerning human relationships and nursing and how the incident relates to nursing, as well as reflect on the significant issues about this incident.
	2. One or two students are asked to share their critical incidents in class. A visual representation of the incident is presented as an 'iceberg' on the white board. Using open questions the student is facilitated to identify and reflect on the emerging issues/themes arising from the incident beyond the surface level of the incident.
	3. Having identified the above, students then undertake a literature search related to the identified themes/issues.
	4. Reflecting on key themes and the relevant literature, the student critically discusses the identified issues and its application to nursing practice.
	5. Group tutorials are offered to help students critically analyse the significant issues and their relevance to nursing and learning. The

Researching

formative aspects of this assessment technique are realized most in these tutorials, where students learn from the teacher and other students through the sharing of experience and related literature. Informal self and peer assessment also takes place and this helps students to reflect on their critical incidents and formulate their own ideas.

6. Students submit a 2000-word critical incident essay, which is summatively assessed.

7. Grading criteria for essays are as follows:
   - a clear beginning, middle and end within 10% of required word limit
   - issues/aims clearly defined and adhered to throughout the paper
   - evidence of a balanced critical discussion of key issues
   - indication of an awareness of the implications for clinical practice
   - evidence of wide reading around the subject
   - application to the practice of nursing
   - evaluation of personal/professional learning
   - full and accurate references and referencing.

Supporting materials	See Guidelines for Identifying Critical Incidents in Appendix.
Outcomes worth noting	☐ Students see this form of assessment as quite different to their usual assessment. They particularly value being able to write about their unique incident and being able to examine components of the incident that are significant to them.
	☐ Students must feel safe and contained within the class if they are to disclose their critical incidents, since some incidents, though useful in increasing self-awareness, can be quite painful. Clarifying issues concerning the limits of confidentiality and establishing a good student-teacher relationship is therefore paramount.
	☐ Students' essays make interesting reading, because each is unique.
Student response	☐ "We need not be restricted to do the topics we don't like. We can choose our incidents that we are interested in and through doing it we can learn to think in different views."
	☐ "(It's) more personal and interesting."
	☐ "It's good to find out about things around us and what is significant to us."
	☐ "Difficult to systematically analyse the incident with theory."
	☐ "This type of assignment is good only if chances for discussion and understanding on the topic are provided."

Researching

How this practice supports learning	• Critical incident analysis supports student-centred learning and provides a framework for learners to develop their ability to think critically, apply theory to practice and increase their awareness both personally and professionally.
	• Using a more student-centred experiential approach may prompt initial feelings of anxiety. Facilitating students in analysing their experience therefore is an important backdrop for its use as an effective and stimulating learning approach.
	• Students develop their abilities not only to analyse and reflect on critical incidents in writing, but also to communicate their ideas and feelings orally to each other, in the tutorials. This is likely to help them to continue to be able to share in an uninhibited way their feelings about critical incidents in their future practice.

Further suggestions	• The self and peer assessment component of this practice could become a formalized, structured part of the process. For example, students could be asked to include a graded self-assessment of their final report, using the same criteria as would be used summatively. This would allow tutor feedback on any significant gaps between students' self-perceptions about their work and the actual quality of the work.
	• As this form of assessment and learning will be new to most students, an opportunity to 'practise' by writing a trial paper or producing a draft on which feedback can be provided could be very helpful for many students. It might be beneficial to have the trial papers peer assessed, for example by two other students, to allow students to learn from each others' strengths and weaknesses, but with brief overall feedback comments also given by the tutor.

Contributor
Jean MORRISSEY
University of Dublin
Email: morrisje@tcd.ie

Researching

APPENDIX

Guidelines for Identifying Critical Incidents

Source: Benner, P. (1984) *From Novice to Expert: Excellence and Power in Clinical Nursing Practice*. Menlo Park, CA: Addison-Wesley.

1.   What constitutes a critical incident

- An incident in which you feel your intervention really made a difference in patient outcome, either directly or indirectly by helping other staff members
- An incident that went unusually well
- An incident in which there was a breakdown (i.e. things did not go as planned)
- An incident that is very ordinary and typical
- An incident that you think captures the quintessence of what nursing is all about
- An incident that was particularly demanding

2.   What to include in the incident

- What was the context of your incident?
- A brief description of what happened
- What makes this incident 'critical' (significant) for you?
- What your concerns were at the time?
- What you were thinking about as it was taking place?
- What were you feeling during and after the incident?

3.   Reflection in and on action

- What is the key issue/theme(s) within the critical incident?
- What have you learnt from this incident?
- How might this incident influence your clinical practice?

Researching

▌ Higher-Order Thinking ▌

5. Using follow-up questions in written assignments

Rocky Yuk Keung FAN, The Open University of Hong Kong

Summary
Where students complete a number of assignments in a subject, later assignments include a question which follows up questions asked in the preceding assignment. This follow-up question is derived from some 'basic' questions asked in the preceding assignment. The basic questions are designed to cover the basic concepts and techniques presented in the course material. Students are motivated to work on at least the follow-up question and the basic questions in each assignment and then study carefully the written comments from their tutors on their answers.

Situations where this practice could be used
This technique can be used when students are required to complete a number of assignments in a subject and the assignments follow a progression so that some matters dealt with in one assignment can be followed up in the subsequent assignment.

Background

This technique has been applied to a first-year distance learning course in applied mathematics. The course has five equal-weighted written assignments and five equal-weighted computer marked assignments for continuous assessment, as well as a final examination. Twenty-five percent of each written assignment, except the first, is allocated to a follow-up question. To pass the course, a student must score at least 40% overall for these assignments.

Rationale

- Many students enrolling in distance learning courses, weaker students in particular, do not submit all the assignments. When assignments are submitted, most students do not study carefully the tutor's comments or work through their mistakes when they are returned.
- Follow-up questions increase the benefit of doing assignments and therefore encourage students to work on at least some questions in each assignment. They provide an opportunity for students to revise the basic concepts and techniques. In addition, if students make mistakes in a basic question, their understanding of the mistakes and tutor comments will be assessed and their improvement will be rewarded by answering the follow-up question.

Higher-Order Thinking

Procedure	1.	The structure and implications of the follow-up questions are explained to students.
	2.	Each written assignment is prepared to include:
		• basic questions — some of which will be followed up in the next assignment (except the last assignment);
		• a follow-up question (except the first assignment). The 'follow-up' question is a modification of one of the original basic questions; and
		• additional questions for further practice of new material.
	3.	Students work on each assignment and submit their answer scripts to tutors for assessment.
	4.	Tutors mark and comment on the answer scripts which are returned to students.
	5.	Students study the tutors' comments on their answer scripts before doing the next assignment.

Supporting materials	☐	None required.

Outcomes worth noting	☐	Submission rates for the written assignments have improved.
	☐	Student performance on the follow-up questions is good.
	☐	Performance of weaker students on additional questions is encouraging.
	☐	Students take the tutor comments on their answers more seriously.
	☐	Using follow-up questions reduces the room for new questions, so it is worth considering the role of optional questions.

Student response	☐	"Using follow-up questions in written assignments is highly recommended."
	☐	"Follow-up questions are good for revision purposes."
	☐	"No follow-up questions. More questions on new material are preferred."
	☐	"Follow-up questions should be harder than the original basic questions."

How this practice supports learning	•	For feedback on an assignment to be truly effective, students need to take notice of the feedback and use it to improve the quality of their work. This practice encourages students to take at least some of the feedback they receive very seriously indeed, since that feedback will help them to answer any 'follow-up' questions on the next assignment. The feedback in this situation clearly works as 'feedforward'.
	•	Students learn how criteria are used for marking and gain a better understanding of how assessment works in practice.

Higher-Order Thinking

Further suggestions	•	Where critical material is covered and assessed early in a module, there are often opportunities to have students review their understanding of it in a subsequent assessment item. In many instances, this could be done with minimal alteration to existing assessment items. The essential pattern of assess — feedback — re-assess could be used with a variety of assessment formats.
	•	Individualized feedback can be time-consuming. The practice could use generic feedback based on common errors made by students.
	•	Students could use the first assignment to practise giving one another peer feedback in order to help them think about how feedback is derived from assessment criteria.

Contributor

Rocky Yuk Keung FAN
School of Science and Technology
The Open University of Hong Kong
Email: rfan@ouhk.edu.hk

6. Same-day feedback and analysis of assessed coursework

Rick GLOFCHESKI, The University of Hong Kong

Summary
Students submit a solution to a hypothetical problem. Later that day, or as soon as possible afterwards, the same problem is discussed in a tutor-led discussion. The tutor then places an 'ideal' solution based on the discussion on the course web site. The process generates critical analysis, reflective discussion, and comparison of the student's submission with the tutor-generated response.

Situations where this practice could be used
- The process could be used in any situation where there is normally a delay in giving feedback on an assignment — perhaps because of class size, the tutor's workload or other factors.
- Since delays in providing feedback are common, this practice could be used in any situation where a lecturer wishes to ensure that students receive quick access to possible solutions to a task to compare with their own submission.
- This procedure could be used in many forms of assessment, including examinations. It will be particularly useful in those courses which employ as a teaching device, problems which require a single, common solution. Teachers in courses such as business, economics, mathematics and physics are likely to find this technique of particular value as a means of reinforcing learning.

Background	☐	The hypothetical problem or case forms the basis of undergraduate law study and final examinations, and normally forms the basis of the weekly tutorial. Tutorial groups are of ten to twelve students in size.
	☐	Students' tutorial preparation consists of assigned text and case readings, and the student's own analysis and 'solution' to the tutorial problem. Tutorials are interactive and encourage students to voice their opinions.
	☐	The assessed exercises mimic the tutorial and the problem/case format. It allows a student to identify errors and to participate in the formulation of an ideal analysis, in the familiar context of a tutorial, but also in the context of assessed coursework, at a time when their own work is still fresh in their minds.
Rationale	☐	The lag time between submission and assessment is unavoidably long when dealing with a large cohort (in this case 250 students). Excessive lag-time diminishes the learning opportunity that assessed coursework affords.
	☐	This simple technique aims to mitigate the effects of lag-time by engaging students in a review of the coursework on a same-day or

Higher-Order Thinking

near same-day basis. Although the formal score and individual written feedback are not yet awarded, students can identify any errors and participate in a critical discussion leading towards the ideal solution.

Procedure	1.	On a fixed date, students submit a solution to a common hypothetical problem/case prepared by the lecturer. The assignment requires students to give 'advice' to the parties who may have been the victim of legal wrongs. A word limit of 700 words is imposed, to mimic the time frame or space typically imposed when answering similar questions in final examinations. A word limit requires a concentration of the mind, as well as the important legal skill of writing concisely.
	2.	Later on the same day of submission (or within two days) the problem is the subject of reflective tutorial discussion led by the tutor. (There are three tutors in the course, including the lecturer.)
	3.	The results of the tutorial discussion, shaped into the form of an ideal solution to the problem, are then posted on the course homepage on the day of submission, providing students with an immediate comparator of their own work.
	4.	A final version of the 'ideal solution', formulated by the lecturer/tutor, is provided to the other tutors, to be followed in the formal assessment and grading process in the weeks to follow.
	5.	Students receive formal feedback and a grade within a few weeks. Students already know where they stand and where they went right or wrong from the tutorial discussion and the comparator solution posted on the course homepage. A review of the individual written feedback will be of as much interest as the grade, which students should be able to predict reasonably accurately.

| **Supporting materials** | ☐ | The comparator solution on the course web site. |

Outcomes worth noting	☐	Oral discussion and group analysis is highly interactive, with wide participation.
	☐	Students adopt a more pensive, focused and engaged approach to discussion.
	☐	Students have the opportunity (albeit limited) to impact on assessment, through principled analysis of and argument about the legal issues, which the lecturer can take into account in formulating the marking guidelines and the posting of the 'solution' on the homepage.
	☐	Students obtain an immediate understanding of the hypothetical problem, avoiding the typical scenario of delayed formal assessment and feedback weeks later, when emphasis is on the score, rather than the substance of the exercise.

Higher-Order Thinking

Student response	☐ "It catches the momentum of students' work asap after submission. (Indeed, it would be ideal if more teachers adopted this approach!) From experience, timely review of coursework in tutorial helps in enhancing my understanding of that material (also in boosting my retention of those topics for a much longer period). Plus, post-tutorial access to the solution on the homepage allows students to focus on the tutorial discussion without the distraction of copying in class. I believe the above benefits will be diminished if the question were not taken up in tutorial, and only later do students get an idea of how well they've grasped this (by then) 'old material'."
	☐ "I think this method of feedback is very effective. Although I found it very stressful in handing in graded assignments, but I think immediate feedback is better than just having answers returned to us since it stimulates our discussion and we can ask questions immediately when we don't understand the concepts. People gather ideas and share and this makes learning very effective. I like this type of tutorial feedback very much."

How this practice supports learning	• Students receive feedback from their peers and tutor within the group discussion. This prompts analysis and assessment of their own work and provides them with a range of perspectives on the one problem.
	• The provision of an 'ideal' solution on the course web site provides a second opportunity for comparison and reflection. It provides a reference point to allow the student to estimate the gap between the quality of their own work and what is required.
	• The initial feedback and discussion focuses on concepts rather than on marks and is provided at a time when the ideas will be fresh in the students' minds, and when they will be highly receptive to thinking about these ideas in the context of their own thoughts (as expressed in their assignment).

Further suggestions	• A simplified version of this practice would involve providing students with the lecturer's own solution as soon as the assignment is handed in. This would not be nearly as effective as discussing the assignment with students beforehand, but when time or the course structure does not allow such discussion to occur quickly enough, the provision of a solution at a time when students are motivated to look at it could still be effective.
	• Although this practice has been found particularly useful in a large group class with multiple tutors, where lag-time in marking is unavoidable, it will work just as well, or better, in a class with one teacher. Such a teacher will have total control over the timing, and

Higher-Order Thinking

can ensure that the classroom discussion takes place immediately after submission, when the ideas are most fresh in students' minds.

Contributor

Rick GLOFCHESKI
Faculty of Law
The University of Hong Kong
Email: rick.glofcheski@hku.hk

7. Quiz-in and quiz-out: A variation of the 'minute paper'

Vicky Kwan Lan TSANG, The Hong Kong Institute of Education

Summary
At the beginning of each class, students respond to a short quiz. At the end of each class, students write some questions or thoughts arising from the class and submit these anonymously. The teacher responds to these during the subsequent class.

Situations where this practice could be used
This practice can be used in any classroom setting.

Background	This technique has been used in teacher education programmes to follow up lecture content.
Rationale	Chinese students are sometimes perceived to be passive learners, partly because reflections are usually carried out silently and students seldom give direct verbal feedback during class. Even when a teacher poses questions during class, only the more extroverted ones tend to answer openly. 'Quiz-in and quiz-out' is a two-way questioning and answering format used during class to serve the following purposes:

□ to provide an alternative channel for asking the teacher questions and soliciting students' feedback during class;

□ to provide an objective way of seeing how much students understand the previous lecture; and

□ to motivate students to review learning from the class that has just taken place.

Procedure	1. In the first class of the module, the teacher explains the purposes and procedures of the quiz time to the entire class.

2. In every class, a ten-minute 'quiz-out' time is slotted into the end of the class time. Each student is asked to write, anonymously, their questions or thoughts about that day's class on a slip of paper.

3. The first ten minutes of each subsequent class is 'quiz-in' time. Each student is tested on a set of five to ten multiple choice questions on topics related to the previous class. A student response system such as 'GoClick' can be used to process responses instantly, making this learning experience more interactive.

4. The teacher responds to the questions from the paper slips collected during the previous class in one way or another during the lecture time so that students can receive teacher responses to their questions.

Higher-Order Thinking

Supporting materials	☐ No special resources are needed for this practice.
	☐ A computer-based 'personal response system' such as 'GoClick' can add an extra dimension to the process by allowing instant processing of students' responses to quizzes.
Outcomes worth noting	☐ Students are encouraged to keep up with their revision so as to help in their knowledge building process.
	☐ An alternative means for two-way teacher-student interactions and feedback is provided.
	☐ The results of the quiz provide extra information on students' understanding, misunderstanding or non-understanding of materials covered.
Student response	☐ "The quiz-out paper slips are good alternatives for me to recollect what my teacher has taught during that class. The beginning quiz-in period helps me to refresh what I have learnt during the previous class."
	☐ "I am shy. I get disorganized in my speech when I have to ask in front of the class. I can express my problems more clearly in writing but not spontaneous speech. I don't have to worry about others knowing that I have asked a stupid question as nobody knows who writes the questions on the paper slip."
	☐ "A test is a test even when it is carried out in a quiz format. There is too much pressure for me when I have to be tested every class. Can we do it just occasionally?"
How this practice supports learning	• This system allows for diagnosis of students' understanding and areas of difficulty. While it is often used at the end of a class to evaluate learning, it could equally well be used at the beginning of a class to see what students know before teaching commences.
	• Feedback to students is quick and immediate if a computer-based system is used. Students are likely to take notice of the feedback, engage in discussion about it, and understand the mistakes they may have made, while coming to appreciate the correct responses.
Further suggestions	• This technique is a variation of the 'minute paper' (Angelo and Cross, 1993).
	• The system can also be used to provide feedback on teaching, to give instant peer feedback on presentations, or to seek student comment on a range of issues.
	• The technique can be used with students in groups, for example in a group verbal quiz competition format, as well as in individual paper quiz format.

Higher-Order Thinking

> - Multiple choice formats, using a student response system, provide a very efficient means of using this technique.
> - For variety, students could be asked to formulate questions for their peers which they slip into the box as they enter the classroom.
> - A 'low-tech' version of 'GoClick' involves using coloured cards that students hold up in response to multiple choice questions.

Reference

Angelo, T. A. and Cross, K. P. (1993) *Classroom Assessment Techniques: A Handbook for College Teachers*. San Francisco: Jossey-Bass.

Contributor

Vicky Kwan Lan TSANG
School of Early Childhood Education
The Hong Kong Institute of Education
Email: vtsang@ied.edu.hk

8. Mini-viva for assignment feedback and discussion

David CARLESS, The University of Hong Kong

Summary

This assessment technique focuses on facilitating prompt verbal dialogue and feedback related to a completed assignment. The form of the discussion is a mini-viva or tutorial where students and tutor engage in a reflective discussion of a completed assignment before a mark is awarded.

Situations where this practice could be used

- This technique could be used in any discipline or situation where students are required to produce an open-ended/discursive piece of written work. It is especially well-suited to project work, but could also be used in conjunction with essays, written critiques, and similar work.
- The technique can be used with group projects.

Background	The mini-viva technique has been used in a module on English language assessment as part of a teacher education programme. It is part of a series of tutorials supporting the development of a group assignment and follows the submission of the assignment. (See Carless, 2002, for a further discussion.)
Rationale	There is often a long time lag between assignment submission and tutor feedback. On receipt of a returned assignment, students may mainly focus on the mark awarded. The mini-viva technique seeks to promote dialogue and reflection on an assignment, after submission, but before a mark is awarded.
Procedure	1. This technique is used as part of a group assignment carried out in groups of three.
	2. Students attend a series of group tutorials focused on the assignment, with the emphasis on clarifying the criteria according to which the work will be graded and giving feedback to students on their work in progress.
	3. Students submit their group assignment.
	4. The tutor quickly reads through the assignments, provisionally marks and grades them and notes some questions which arise.
	5. A fifteen-minute group tutorial in the form of a mini-viva is held. Students respond to tutor comments and questions about their assignment, and receive feedback.
	6. After the mini-viva, the tutor finalizes grades in the normal way.

Higher-Order Thinking

Supporting materials	None required. The assignment description is attached for reference (Appendix).
Outcomes worth noting	☐ The practice facilitates prompt dialogue and feedback concerning the assignment. ☐ The interactive nature of the oral discussion of the assignment in the mini-viva is more educational and satisfying than purely written feedback which may be only partially understood or not engaged with. ☐ Through questioning, the tutor has the opportunity to monitor individual student contributions to the group assignment. ☐ The tutor gains useful information concerning what students have really achieved. This can contribute to a fairer assessment of students' learning. ☐ The process enables the tutor to form an opinion about the relative contributions and understandings of individual members of a group project, which *may* be used to adjust individual grades. (This should be done cautiously, as reliable judgements are often difficult in a short group interview.)
Student response	☐ "We get feedback quickly rather than having to wait for a long time for the marking." ☐ "I like the feedback sessions as we could learn from them how we did the assignment and it's a chance to clarify any unclear issues." ☐ "For some points when you didn't understand why we wrote in a certain way, we can explain it to you." ☐ "The tutorial process is quite useful but I would prefer to know the mark during or immediately after the tutorial. It seemed a bit cruel not to be told the mark until a few days after the tutorial."
How this practice supports learning	• The mini-viva can help students to consolidate, extend and integrate their learning through reflection on the work that they have produced. It is likely to be more effective than written comments, especially since these are often largely ignored by students when they are given on final assignments. • With written feedback, the 'production-to-consumption' ratio is high. That is, it takes a long time to compose good feedback, and because it is not interactive, points cannot be clarified or elaborated. The provider has to anticipate the learner's 'feedback needs'. Students tend to give written feedback, no matter how carefully composed, only cursory attention. • Verbal feedback can be given much more quickly, and is consequently likely to be given more attention by students.

Higher-Order Thinking

Further suggestions	• The mini-viva itself could be assessed, with a proportion of marks (say 20%) allocated to it.
	• The mini-viva could be conducted on an individual basis. This may be important if marks are being allocated to it. Individual vivas would be time-consuming, but they can be quite short and often have a significant impact on student learning as they prepare for them.
	• Following the viva, students could be required to revise their assignment, including a reflective response to issues raised in the viva and how they have improved their assignment in light of these issues.
	• Where there are multiple assignments in a module, the oral feedback given in the mini-viva could replace rather than complement the written feedback for one assignment.

Reference

Carless, D. (2002) The 'mini-viva' as a tool to enhance assessment for learning. *Assessment and Evaluation in Higher Education, 27*(4), 353–63.

Contributor

David CARLESS
The University of Hong Kong
Email: dcarless@hkucc.hku.hk

APPENDIX

Summative Assignment

Task.   Design a portfolio of informal and formal assessment tools for the primary ESL classroom. Explain the rationale for the assessment tools/items. Indicate the relationship between the assessments and pupil learning.

Organization and procedures.   Work in a group of three. Indicate clearly on the assignment, the responsibilities of each member of the group, as you will receive one individual mark (40% weighting) and one group mark (60% weighting). After the submission of the assignment, I will mark the portfolio and award a provisional grade. I will invite the group for a tutorial and will ask questions to clarify any queries about the assignment and the respective individual student contributions. Final grades will be awarded after these tutorials.

Higher-Order Thinking

9. 'Asking a question': A time-saving assessment tool

Lilian L. P. VRIJMOED, City University of Hong Kong

Summary
At the end of a class, students are required to submit a question based on the content of that lecture/laboratory session/tutorial within a week. These questions become the basis for class and online discussion. This discussion provides timely feedback to students and also allows an opportunity for students to learn from one another, both in terms of content knowledge and reflective/critical thinking. The questions are graded as part of the students' assessment.

Situations where this practice could be used
This technique could be used in almost any discipline where assignments need to be short and effective. It discourages plagiarism and is especially suitable for assessing large classes.

Background	Passive learners are usually surface learners who are not likely to reflect on what they have learned. In order to facilitate deeper learning and transform students' 'memorized' information into functional knowledge, 'asking a question' has been turned into an assignment and a learning exercise at the same time in some undergraduate major courses in applied biology.
Rationale	Passive learners can become engaged in learning when they are required to ask a question on the content covered during a class. How the question is phrased indicates the level of understanding and reflection by the students on that content. This practice seeks to □ develop active, reflective learning skills; □ provide timely feedback; and □ encourage collaborative learning.
Procedure	1. After completing the delivery of a specific part of the syllabus, an assignment is set in the form of 'asking a question' within one week. For example, following a lecture on fungi, a student may ask, 'What features distinguish fungi from the plants and animal kingdom?' 2. All the submitted questions are then grouped into different categories by the teacher to facilitate discussion. 3. Questions are made 'public' (with the names of students hidden) and discussed in class. This discussion process facilitates timely feedback and consolidation of content knowledge. The questions provide the lecturer with information about what remains to be addressed in terms of student learning. 4. The discussion process is also designed to enhance understanding of what makes a good question. The way a question is framed and worded

Higher-Order Thinking

reflects the level of understanding of the topic being dealt with as well as the depth of student learning.

5. If there are too many questions, the less important ones can be transferred to an online platform for discussion.

6. Grading or formal marking of questions can be deferred until students have some practice and are familiar with what is required. In other words, early assignments can be 'formative' until students are comfortable with the subject area, then 'summative' assignments can be introduced. Bloom's 'taxonomy of educational objectives' can be used to identify the indicative verbs in the learning outcomes and assign appropriate 'weightings' accordingly.

7. Maximal value could be added when the questions are rearranged to form an FAQ (frequently asked questions) bank and self-assessment exercises are designed for weaker learners.

Supporting materials	None required.
Outcomes worth noting	☐ Students often do more than what is required — they pose more questions on the online discussion forum.
	☐ Weak students are identified in time and can be helped to improve their performance well before other forms of assessment.
	☐ Teachers obtain valuable and timely feedback on which areas the students are generally finding most difficult to grasp.
	☐ Students engage in the highly valuable learning process of metacognition which encourages them to engage in deep learning.
Student response	☐ "Asking a question really makes me think about what I have learned in class. The process makes me realize what I 'think' I understand and know may not really mean I really understand."
	☐ "I learn a lot from the questions asked by my classmates because from those questions, I know there are many aspects of the content knowledge that I never thought of."
	☐ "Asking questions makes me think about what I have learned. Now I have a deeper understanding of the topics taught in class, I have more confidence in dealing with open book tests and examinations."
	☐ "My workload increases because having to generate questions takes more time and makes me think too hard."
	☐ "Making me think up questions is difficult and means there are too many assignments."

How this practice supports learning	This practice supports learning in a number of ways: • It spreads student effort throughout the module, without overloading students or creating a heavy marking load. • It encourages a collaborative learning environment where students have the opportunity to develop a more inquisitive and reflective mind. • Posing a question requires student to review what has been taught. It typically requires them to process information at a deeper level than is required by simply *responding to* a question.

Further suggestions	• Students can be introduced to the criteria being used — the taxonomy for learning, teaching and assessment itself can be an explicit focus of discussion. (See Anderson and Krathwohl, 2001.) • All questions could be placed on the online discussion forum to encourage students to pose questions that are relevant to their peers and to identify issues of common concern or interest. • Students could be invited, in groups, to respond to the questions — either in class or online with the teacher subsequently providing elaboration or clarification. • Another suggestion from the contributor is that students can be asked to generate their own list of five questions before a lecture or tutorial and submit them online to a discussion board. They then write a short paragraph after the class examining the extent to which they have answers to their questions and which questions remain unanswered. • Allocating marks based on the quality of questions asked may be difficult to do fairly in many situations. The practice could be used without marks being given. If marks are allocated, these should be limited.

Reference

Anderson, L. W. and Krathwohl, D. R. (eds). (2001) *A Taxonomy for Learning, Teaching, and Assessing.* New York: Longman.

Contributor

Lilian L. P. VRIJMOED
City University of Hong Kong
Email: bhlilian@cityu.edu.hk

Higher-Order Thinking

▌ Communicating Using Technology ▌

Communicating Using Technology

10. Using online processes to enhance assessment and learning

Eliza K. O. AU, The Hong Kong Institute of Education

Summary
This assessment technique focuses on using online processes in an art education module. The module was redesigned to utilize authentic assessment strategies, including the following elements: tasks for formative assessment; a discussion board using the Blackboard online learning management system; real-life situations in problem-based learning; constructivist learning in identifying what students need to know through group negotiation; and group work in collaborative learning.

Situations where this practice could be used
This practice integrates a number of techniques within a problem-based learning approach to teaching a module. These techniques can be used:
- when problem-based learning approaches are being applied;
- to promote debate between groups of students; or
- to provide a dynamic environment for peer and lecturer feedback.

Background   The *Art Education* foundation module in which this practice was developed introduces the historical, social, cultural and psychological underpinnings of art education. It allows education students to understand why some ideas in today's art education are valued, how the field of education relates to students' holistic learning, how it reflects their cultural identity, and how it has been defined as a result of consideration of important social issues.

Rationale   How a lecturer should introduce the complexity of art education theories to a group of first year pre-service teachers raises many critical issues. Direct teaching has relatively little impact on students as the theories presented are often presented as given — the body of knowledge is predetermined by the lecturer and becomes the curriculum that is 'delivered'. The assessment tasks are then designed to determine if the theories can be applied in practice. Because of these limitations, the art education module has been redesigned to utilize authentic assessment strategies to encourage constructivist and collaborative learning.

Procedure   1.   The module lecturer uses digital images of Cosplayers (costume players who dress up as their favourite animated or video-game characters) and videos of teacher interviews as triggers for problem-based learning

(PBL). From the cases presented, participants work in groups to identify learning issues for further inquiry. Examples of the issues that might be identified are "Why are teenagers attracted to popular culture?", "How is school art different from popular art?", and "Identifying teaching conceptions through personal metaphors".

2. The class is divided into small groups of four to five students. From the PBL cases, each group identifies the learning issues they want to pursue. Students are encouraged to use technology as a tool for investigation and documentation. For example, they may search the Internet for information, solicit youngsters' views on visual culture by means of a web survey, record students' work using digital cameras and videotape their interviews with teachers and the visual environment of the school.

3. Each group presents their learning issues in class. Students can choose their presentation format. Some groups, for example, may use PowerPoint, while others may use role-play, debate and simulations to present their study. The group presentation provides the base for collaboration and constructive learning. The students decide the issues they want to learn. They also decide their roles in the group, whether as group leader, scribe, researcher, designer or presenter.

4. After the presentation, the data, images and videos are uploaded to an online discussion board in *Blackboard*. The students write responses to the issues identified by individual groups, and debate controversial views, e.g. the strength of fine-arts-based versus visual-culture-based curriculum or the metaphor for an art teacher, i.e. whether an art teacher is just like a farmer or a shepherd. Students and the module lecturer can provide feedback to the whole group or individually.

5. The online discussion provides a platform for sharing and critiquing of ideas on curriculum, teaching and learning. Through feedback and responses, students begin to see perspectives of their peers and the module lecturer. They can make changes to their initial writing and submit the responses as part of the formative assessment.

6. The summative assessment is an individual essay on teaching visual culture in secondary school. Students can make reference to the presentation and discussion when working on their final assignment.

Supporting materials	☐ Digital images from newspapers, magazines, the local environment and the Internet
	☐ Case videos on Cosplay and teacher conceptions of art teaching
	☐ Journal articles for reading and response
Outcomes worth noting	☐ The use of cases in problem-based learning is very effective in developing skills in self-directed learning. These skills involve identification of learning issues, the use of information sources from

Communicating Using Technology

the Internet and community, and the application of newly acquired knowledge and skills to teaching and learning. The use of *Blackboard* helps students to discuss the issues beyond their own groups. The responses and feedback from peers and the module lecturer are easily accessible anytime and anywhere.

☐ The design of formative assessment tasks in the discussion board helps students to start thinking and debating about the issues throughout the module. The summative assessment is no longer a last-minute task before the deadline.

Student response	☐ "We felt less pressured. It's just like studying for interest, so I like this kind of formative assessment." ☐ "We could document our idea for the assignment whenever, wherever, and we could always make changes to that before the submission deadline. Also we could read and comment on classmates' assignments and responses on the platform." ☐ "I think group work is important in tertiary education and group assignments can train us on this aspect."
How this practice supports learning	• The structure of this module and its assessment ensures that students work consistently over time. Their involvement in deciding on the focus of their work is likely to increase their commitment to their learning. • The group nature of the work is an opportunity to develop skills in teamwork. • Opportunities for feedback and ongoing discussion on the web site are timely and allow for revision of the final essay. • Students are able to include their responses to feedback in their final submission. This ensures that they take note of the feedback and actively use it to improve their work. The invitation to explicitly refer to online discussion in their assignment also encourages students' active engagement in this discussion. • Seeing and critiquing others' work heightens students' awareness of standards and helps develop their ability to evaluate their own work. • Having to make work available to others on the web site gives incentive to produce good quality work.
Further suggestions	• Explicit discussion of standards would enable students to more readily evaluate their own and their peers' work. • A self-evaluation process could be included in the summative assessment to invite students to reflect on the quality of their work

Communicating Using Technology

and their learning in the module. (This would not necessarily include self-*grading*.)

- A short additional written task could ask students to reflect on the *emergent* learning outcomes of the overall work, i.e. what were the most useful things they had learned as a result of the way the work was structured and assessed.

Contributor
Eliza K. O. AU
Department of Creative Arts
The Hong Kong Institute of Education
Email: koau@ied.edu.hk

11. Peer assessment using electronic reflective journals

Ada Wai Wing MA and Eugenia Mee Wah NG, The Hong Kong Institute of Education

Summary
This practice fosters collaborative learning by engaging learners in peer assessment of group work. Student groups devise their own assessment criteria. By conducting peer assessment on the web, instant feedback is available.

Situations where this practice could be used
This practice could be used wherever assessment, and associated learning is based on a group project.

Background	This practice has been used in a first-year textile science module within a Bachelor of Education programme.
Rationale	Peer learning is one of the many learner-centred approaches that match the philosophy of contemporary perspectives on learning and teaching which aim to promote higher achievement, more positive interpersonal relationships and improved psychological health.
Procedure	1. Peer groups arrive at an agreed set of assessment criteria that are then posted onto a module web page.
	2. Learners conduct an intra-group reflection that forms the basis of the growth of the group by critically analysing their progress (learning processes) as well as giving suggestions on strategies to enhance the group's effectiveness through submission of an electronic bi-weekly reflective journal.
	3. Learners perform an inter-group assessment by giving feedback and grades to their peers' project presentations and report at the end of the semester via the Web to advance and demonstrate their lateral thinking skills.
	4. Learners receive prompt feedback from both the lecturer and their peers.
Supporting materials	□ Bi-weekly reflective journals and project presentations and reports are uploaded to the module web site for sharing and critique (Appendix 1).
	□ A peer assessment pro forma is provided (Appendix 2).
Outcomes worth noting	□ Learners have expressed very positive and favourable reflections on their performance. They have been satisfied with the team collaboration and they believe they have learnt a lot from their team mates.

Communicating Using Technology

□ The total scores for different groups given by both peer groups and lecturer fall in the same grade according to the formal marking scheme, but learners, in general, have been more lenient in marking their peers' work.

□ Learners have had positive perceptions of using online peer assessment in assessing group project work.

□ Learners have perceived that peer assessment is able to foster collaborative learning effectively.

Student response	□ "At (the end) we would have to mark three assignments. By comparing them, we could easily tell which one was good. Being the marker, I could also learn the good things from others' work. To mark others' work, we have to learn to be critical."
	□ "I think peer assessment allows group members to discuss thoroughly before assigning marks since we should give neutral comments."
	□ "Through peer assessment, we could practice our marking technique. To objectively criticize others' work without hurting others' feeling, this is what we have learnt."
	□ "The workload is huge and it's time-consuming to conduct the inter-group peer assessment. Having said that, it provides us a golden opportunity to learn collaboratively."

How this practice supports learning	• Deriving a set of assessment criteria helps students come to grips with what is expected in a module. It also helps them to appreciate the criteria and standards that they need to strive for and that are relevant in judging their own work.
	• Students have a greater sense of ownership of criteria they have developed themselves, and are therefore likely to apply the criteria more objectively to each others' work.
	• Assessment by peer groups, rather than by individual peers, promotes discussion about criteria and standards, thereby helping students develop a clearer understanding of these.

Further suggestions	• Feedback, possibly by peers, on a preliminary or draft report would allow an opportunity to revise work.
	• Students could be asked to self-assess their own work, and then compare their self-assessments with that of their peers, and discuss any significant differences which may be found.

Contributors

Ada Wai Wing MA and Eugenia Mee Wah NG
Department of Mathematics, Science, Social Sciences and Technology
The Hong Kong Institute of Education
Email: ama@ied.edu.hk; eugenia@ied.edu.hk

Communicating Using Technology

APPENDIX 1

Module Title: Textile Science

Lecturer:

Peer Assessment

(A)   Group Processing — Bi-weekly Reflective Journal

(Submission of bi-weekly reflective journal is a prerequisite for completion of the module. Members of each group are required to conduct self-assessment first which would be followed by intra-group sharing and proposed improved course of actions.)

Group no. : _____
Members and their registration nos.: _____ (   )
_____ (   )
_____ (   )

Items to be assessed	Excellent (A)	Good (B)	Satisfactory (C)	Fair (D)	Fail (E)
(1) Performance on knowledge sharing					
• Ability to explain, discuss and teach what they know to teammates					
• Ability to promote interactive discussion					
(2) Contribution to learning processes (Collaboration)					
• Leadership					
• Decision-making					
• Trust-building					
• Interactive communication					
• Negotiation and conflict management					
• Contribution to learning processes (Reflection)					
• Capacity to reflect critically					
• Capacity to provide useful feedback					
• Openness to feedback					
Overall comment and suggestions for improvement:					

APPENDIX 2

(B) Peer Assessment

(Learner and lecturer input will be weighted at 30% and 70% respectively.)

Group no.: _____
Group no. to be assessed: _____

Items to be assessed	Excellent (A)	Good (B)	Satisfactory (C)	Fair (D)	Fail (E)
• Ability to understand the requirement of the task (20%)					
• Accuracy of analysis • Appropriateness of conclusions drawn (20%)					
• Depth of research (20%)					
• Organization of presentation (20%)					
• Clarity of expression • Appropriate use of IT to support presentation (20%)					
Total					

Overall comment and suggestions for improvement:

12. Providing immediate feedback through a 'personal response system'

Harrison TSE, The Hong Kong Institute of Education

Summary

This practice involves the use of 'GoClick' — a 'personal response system' that uses infrared technology to enable individual students to answer multiple-choice questions by selecting and clicking buttons on hand-held wireless transmitters. A receiver picks up the data, stores and analyses it for immediate display.

Situations where this practice could be used

- This practice can be used in any classroom setting where a lecturer wants to pose questions to which all students can respond. The capacity to process responses immediately creates a powerful feedback tool, as well as providing data for ongoing class discussion.
- The system provides a highly efficient alternative to end-of-class paper-and-pencil tests.

Background	The tactic has been used for two groups of final-year education students studying a module on assessment.
Rationale	Marking multiple-choice responses is often a task that requires considerable time and effort by lecturers. The use of personal response systems such as 'GoClick' makes this process automatic, along with the provision of immediate feedback to a class that is using such a system.
Procedure	1. 'GoClick' needs to be installed on the lecturer's laptop or on the classroom computer. 2. Students are told that their learning will be evaluated before the end of the class. 3. At the end of the class, individual students are asked to answer ten multiple-choice questions on topics they have just learnt by selecting and clicking the buttons on the hand-held wireless transmitters assigned to them. 4. The results of the multiple-choice assessment are analysed and displayed on the projected screen. 5. Students' responses to specific questions and the suggested answers become the focus of class comments, suggestions and discussion. 6. The results are saved on the computer. If appropriate, the progress of individual students over several tests can be recorded.
Supporting materials	'GoClick' (or any other personal response system), which includes hand-held wireless transmitters and a receiver. The system has to be installed and connected to a computer in the classroom.

Communicating Using Technology

Outcomes worth noting	☐ Immediate feedback on the multiple-choice assessment makes it easy for individual students to identify their own scores, the scores of their groups and/or the scores of the class as a whole.
	☐ The application of technology allows students to monitor their own progress and to enhance their sense of responsibility for their own learning.

Student response	☐ "Very convenient (to use)!"
	☐ "It may lead to stress in student learning because assessment can be carried out frequently."
	☐ "It allows every one of us to participate and we can know the results of assessment instantly."
	☐ "Interesting. It encourages students to evaluate (their own learning)."
	☐ "It reduces teacher's workload. Reduction in the time for processing. For those who are interested in using computers, the technology enhances their learning motivation."

How this practice supports learning	• This system allows for instant diagnosis of students' understanding and areas of difficulty. While it is often used at the end of a class to test learning, it could equally well be used at the beginning of a class to see what students know before teaching commences.
	• Feedback to students is immediate. Because of this, students are likely to take notice of the feedback, engage in discussion about it, and understand the mistakes they may have made, while coming to appreciate the correct responses.
	• It is difficult for a student to hide passively in a large group, since each individual must respond.

Further suggestions	• The system can also be used to provide instant feedback on teaching; prompt peer feedback on presentations; encourage debate on contentious topics and issues; and seek student comment on a range of issues.
	• Low-tech versions using colour cards that students hold up in response to oral questions can be used where the technology is unavailable.

Contributor

Harrison TSE
Department of Curriculum and Instruction
The Hong Kong Institute of Education
htse@ied.edu.hk

Communicating Using Technology

13. An electronic feedback bank

Pamela LEUNG, The Hong Kong Institute of Education

Summary
Feedback items adopted for a particular subject reflect the assessment criteria as well as the learning objectives. An electronic database facilitates prompt feedback on various aspects of a piece of assessment. Tutors can fine-tune their exact expectations and inform students by commenting on drafts before the final submission.

Situations where this practice could be used
Electronic feedback processes can be applied to most forms of assessment in most disciplines.

Background	This practice was developed for use in teaching Chinese to education students.
Rationale	Assessment requirements are often embedded in assignment guidelines. Tutors may not recognize the importance of conveying their exact expectations to students until they are disappointed by poor work from students. Developing a feedback bank which includes indicators of different performance levels is a way of establishing an explicit set of assessment criteria, thus highlighting what is most important in learning, for both tutors and students. Using an electronic mode allows for easy updating and efficient online operation.
Procedure	1. The tutor drafts a preliminary set of feedback comments according to assessment criteria. This can be done in a number of ways. (See 'Supporting Materials' below.) 2. Students are invited to submit their draft assignments for feedback. This step is not compulsory. Submission is by email or via the Blackboard learning management system. 3. The tutor reads the drafts, adds appropriate feedback and returns the drafts to students. 4. As the tutor provides feedback on the draft, the feedback is added to a 'feedback bank'. This feedback bank is progressively revised and enriched from the feedback provided to all students. At the end of this stage, a comprehensive feedback bank has been formulated to support the formal assessment. 5. Students use the tutor feedback to improve their drafts or seek further clarification from the tutor about the appropriate follow-up action. They can submit further drafts if they wish and again receive feedback. 6. The tutor revises the feedback set based on these further drafts, adding

additional items to reflect the strengths and weaknesses in student performances, and enriches the set of suggestions for improvement.

7. On the final assignment, the tutor uses feedback items from the expanded feedback bank, inserting these as appropriate in the students' assignments. Additional comments specific to each particular assignment are added when necessary.

8. As well as inserting feedback at specific points in a student's work, a summary statement is added at the end of the assignment. This is generated automatically from the individual feedback statements, but is revised and added to by the tutor.

Note: The feedback bank can be created using categories based on assessment criteria and standards. This is particularly important when the bank reaches a large number of items which would then need be categorized so that they can be accessed easily.

Supporting materials	☐ An electronic feedback bank can be built using a range of database software, e.g., commonly used software such as Excel. Endnote has been used because it supports Chinese characters and can generate a detailed list of comments at the end of a document.
	☐ Proprietary software programmes are also available for this purpose.
Outcomes worth noting	☐ Prompt feedback can be given concerning the various aspects of assignment requirements.
	☐ Feedback items can be fine-tuned or modified easily.
	☐ The bank of items, and the process of developing it, facilitates tutor reflection on his or her own thinking and practices.
	☐ Supplementary face-to-face consultation may still be needed as students may not fully understand the written comments.
Student response	☐ "We became more confident that we were on the right track when we learned from your prompts that our initial attempts were acceptable."
	☐ "We compared and discussed the similar remarks you provided on different essays. This allowed us to see what you expected from different examples."
	☐ "Although we did not understand fully what the feedback meant, we knew (where) our problems were in the draft essay."
How this practice supports learning	• Detailed feedback can be provided efficiently and quickly once the data bank has been created. If a tutor is teaching the same module on repeated occasions, the technique becomes increasingly workload efficient.

Communicating Using Technology

- Comments can be created to ensure that they are closely related to criteria and standards.
- Comments can be drafted carefully so that they are more likely to be understood by students.
- The process of creating a bank of comments leads tutors to think carefully about the nature of good feedback and the feedback process.

| **Further suggestions** | • This practice generates feedback but does not deal with how that feedback is used. Other processes can be used to supplement this, for example processes that strongly encourage students to act on feedback provided. This applies particularly to a final assignment, where high quality feedback may not impact on student learning unless they use it in later work. |

Contributor

Pamela LEUNG
Department of Chinese
The Hong Kong Institute of Education
Email: pleung@ied.edu.hk

▮ Communicating Orally or in Writing ▮

14. Engaging students in critical discussion of assignments

CHEUNG Siu Kau, City University of Hong Kong

Summary
Before a tutorial, students submit their tutorial assignment and prepare a PowerPoint file based on the assignment answers to present in the tutorial. In the tutorial, students can volunteer to present their assignment answers or the tutor draws lots to determine the presenter. Assessment of student participation is based on the frequency and quality of questions or comments they make in the tutorial. Students thus receive feedback on their answers from their peers and are better able to master the concepts involved. The tutor assesses the assignments (which have been submitted through WebCT) and gives individualized comments to students within two weeks.

Situations where this practice could be used
This practice can be used in many disciplines and whenever students are required to make presentations of their assignments.

Background	This practice has been used in associate degree social science courses.
Rationale	When students are responsible for a topic and present this in a tutorial, other students in the group may not be well enough prepared to understand and comment on the presentation. They may also be too absorbed in mentally rehearsing their own presentation to listen to others. Feedback thus often comes mainly from the tutor, with students not engaged in giving feedback or in discussion. This practice has been developed to overcome these problems and to encourage deep engagement during discussion of assignment questions. The practice
	☐ encourages students to submit high-quality assignments;
	☐ prepares students for critical discussion of assignment questions; and
	☐ encourages peer feedback and active discussion of assignment questions.
Procedure	*Before the tutorial*
	1. Case situations or discussion topics are set for tutorials following lectures. For each tutorial, there is usually one set case followed by five or six questions. Students can download the required material from the course web site (WebCT).
	2. All students respond to the same questions and submit their answers to the web site before the tutorial. Students also summarize their answers in a PowerPoint file and must be ready to present this in the tutorial.

In the tutorial

3. The tutor invites volunteers or draws lots to decide who will be the 'presenter' of a question. The presenter projects his or her PowerPoint slides, but is not required to explain them.

4. The tutor facilitates discussion by inviting the other students to raise questions or give comments. The presenter is required to respond to these questions, often clarifying what they have presented. The tutor invites others to join the discussion.

5. If no one raises questions or comments, the tutor directs questions to the other students (not to the presenter).

6. Students other than the presenter are also encouraged to share their own answers to the first question with the class.

7. Once the students seem to understand the concepts involved in the first question, the tutor moves on to another question — and another student is invited to act as the presenter.

8. During the tutorial, the tutor records the frequency and quality of students' participation, which serves as the basis for assessing participation.

9. Assessment of students' participation in tutorials is based on their performance in asking questions and giving comments. Those who sit through a tutorial without saying anything will only get 20%. Those who raise one comment or ask one question will be given 40%. Only those who participate actively or give a presentation will get 60% or more. Both frequency and quality of the participation will be counted.

After the tutorial

10. The tutor will mark the WebCT submissions and give supplementary individualized comments for students within two weeks.

Supporting materials	☐	A series of cases and questions.
	☐	A learning management system such as WebCT or BlackBoard provides an efficient way for students to submit their work and for feedback to be provided.
Outcomes worth noting	☐	Many students volunteer to present their answers, because being the presenter in a tutorial guarantees 60% of the participation score.
	☐	Students usually feel satisfied and relieved at the end of the tutorial.
	☐	Students contribute actively to discussion.
	☐	Students acquire an understanding of the concepts and issues.
Student response	☐	"I am not afraid of presenting my answers any more because it is just sharing."
	☐	"We are all prepared for the same questions, and we can really exchange our ideas on the assignment".
	☐	"I can really grasp the concepts before the lectures proceed."

Communicating Orally or in Writing

How this practice supports learning	This practice supports student learning in several ways:
	• Students are required to work on all of the tutorial topics across the semester since they have to submit their answers to questions for each of the tutorials.
	• The requirement to condense their responses into a PowerPoint file will get them to 'think twice' about their responses — the process of producing a succinct summary often requires a greater understanding of a topic than writing in a looser format.
	• Students are likely to prepare well for each tutorial since there is always a possibility that they will be asked to present. Of course, students who have already presented may not engage as thoroughly with the topics of forthcoming tutorials, as their marks then would be likely to be restricted to participation rather than presentation.
	• Students often tend to seek a deeper understanding of a topic when they know that they will be asked questions about it.

Further suggestions	• To reduce the marking load, the tutor could mark only the presenters' submissions. Students who do not present then assess each other's work in pairs and give feedback based on criteria. This process allows the 'non-presenting' students to learn from considering a peer's work, as well as from the feedback they receive. The peer assessment process helps to ensure that the work is done while also promoting learning. This would also reduce any tendency for those who had already presented to do less work for forthcoming tutorials.
	• Awarding marks according to the quantity of contributions may not suit all tutors. A focus on the quality of contributions is usually important, but does require more tutor time.
	• Simply being present does not demonstrate achievement. It may be worth considering awarding marks to a student only when a contribution is made.
	• It may be worth considering having a few marks for each tutorial reserved for individual self-assessments of the contribution students made to the tutorial, with the possibility of the tutor intervening if students who had not contributed tried to award themselves these marks.

Communicating Orally or in Writing

Contributor

CHEUNG Siu Kau

City University of Hong Kong

Email: s.k.cheung@cityu.edu.hk

15. Providing and receiving feedback on writing tasks

Emily Po Sheung YAN and Vivian Yuk Yi LI, The Chinese University of Hong Kong

Summary
This technique aims to enhance students' awareness and performance in writing effectively by engaging them in providing and receiving feedback in peer review exercises and discussion meetings throughout the semester. Students are trained to understand and use the review forms on which performance objectives for good writing are clearly articulated prior to the peer review. Based on the feedback, students revise and improve the assignments before they submit them for grading.

Situations where this practice could be used
This process could be used in short writing tasks. The general process of peer review using given criteria can be applied to most disciplines, especially where the task does not count towards a final mark.

Background	In an undergraduate English writing course, students are required to write five short (two pages) in-class assignments and two longer (four to six pages) homework assignments in a semester. Prior to the submission of each paper for grading, a peer review exercise is conducted to allow students to give and receive feedback for revision and improvement of the assignment.
Rationale	Students are motivated to write and revise better when □ they are well informed of the criteria for good performance; □ they are actively involved in giving and receiving feedback on their performance; and □ they receive immediate feedback from readers (peers).
Procedure	1. Students are given guidelines with clearly articulated performance objectives for reviewing writing assignments. The criteria are thoroughly explained to students to ensure proper understanding. 2. Students try out the review process with the help of the assessment scheme, peer review form and sample assignments. The teacher discusses the sample assignments with the class and how they should be reviewed. 3. To conduct the review exercise: • Students form pairs according to their own preference. They will have a different partner in different exercises. • They are allotted fifteen minutes for reviewing class work (about two pages) and twenty to twenty-five minutes for homework assignments of about four to six pages in length.

Communicating Orally or in Writing

- Students are asked to provide formative feedback both on the scripts and by answering questions on the peer review forms.
4. Students conduct short discussion meetings to elaborate on comments as necessary, answer queries and address concerns.
5. Students revise their work and submit it to their teacher for grading, along with the peer review form.

Supporting materials	□	The assessment scheme for writing activities (Appendix 1).
	□	The peer evaluation form (Appendix 2 shows a sample that students use in reviewing descriptive writing).

Outcomes worth noting	□	Students are highly motivated to write and revise their work.
	□	Their improved attitude leads to improved performance.
	□	Students are more critical about their own performance when they are asked to evaluate the performance of others.
	□	An important by-product is improved social skills in providing and accepting feedback.

Student response	□	"I think twice before I write."
	□	"I proofread before I hand in my work, from different perspectives: content, language and organization."
	□	"I do not want to make my friends angry and just say something nice."

How this practice supports learning	•	Students often seem to work harder on an assignment when they know it will be read by a fellow student and then discussed with them.
	•	Students gain feedback from a wider range of perspectives than just from a tutor, allowing them deeper reflection on their ongoing writing.
	•	The review process engages students with the criteria for good work and helps them develop a sense of the standard required.
	•	Students are better able to monitor the quality of their own work when they have critiqued the work of others.
	•	Students are enabled to learn from the best practices of their peers, and also to avoid in their own work the weaknesses they identify in their peers' work.

Further suggestions	•	Students could be involved in generating criteria and standards. This may help students to find out more about which assessment criteria work well in the assessment of their work, and which criteria are more difficult to use in practice.
	•	A self-review process could be applied to the students' revised work prior to submission.

Communicating Orally or in Writing

> • Students could be asked to reflect on any differences between their self-assessment of their work and the assessment by their peers. This reflection could contribute to the overall assessment of their work.

Contributors

Emily Po Sheung YAN and Vivian Yuk Yi LI
The Chinese University of Hong Kong
Email: emilyan@cuhk.edu.hk; vivianli@cuhk.edu.hk

APPENDIX 1

Assessment scheme for writing activities

	Content	*Language*	*Organization*
A A–	• Task requirement fully fulfilled • Main ideas are clearly stated with relevant ideas presented logically • Purpose very effectively achieved • Very good sense of audience	• Absence of or infrequent errors in spelling, punctuation, sentence structure and word usage and expression. • A wide range and variety of vocabulary and structure • Very good use of tone	• Well-structured presentation and development of topic • Transitions are always marked appropriately.
B+ B B–	• Task requirement fulfilled • Always communicates intended meaning with little extra effort required on the part of the reader • Purpose achieved • Clear sense of audience	• Reasonably accurate in the use of language forms • An adequate range and variety of vocabulary and structures • Shows attention to the use of appropriate tone	• Clear and logical development of topic • Appropriate transitions between ideas and paragraphs
C+ C C–	• Task requirement partially fulfilled • Text largely comprehensible with meaning sometimes obscured • Purpose somehow unclear • Insufficient understanding of audience	• Frequent errors in grammar and sentence constructions • A limited range and variety of vocabulary and structures • Improper use of tone	• Unclear structure of presentation • Organization sometimes interferes with communication of ideas
D+ D	• Fails to address the task requirement • Intended meanings are obscured • Purpose not clear • Fails to show an understanding of audience	• Very frequent grammatical errors and poor use of language forms • Inappropriate tone	• Incoherent structure of presentation • Poor organization that always interferes with communication of ideas
F	• Wrong interpretation of the task requirement • Intended meanings are always obscured • Purpose very unclear • Wrong understanding of audience	• Dominated by grammatical errors and language forms • Wrong tone	• Illogical structure • Fails to organize the text

Remarks:

Communicating Orally or in Writing

APPENDIX 2

Peer Review of Writing Exercises

Class: _____   Assignment: _____

Name of writer: _____   Name of reviewer: _____

This peer review exercise enables you to collaborate and stimulate each other with ideas for revising and improving on the writing assignment. You will read each other's work at least twice.

Read your classmate's paper and make brief notes on problems you may find in the first reading. Before you read your classmate's paper again, read the following questions:

1. What are the requirements of this essay? Has the work fulfilled the task requirements? Elaborate your response.
2. Do you understand the main ideas of this work? What are they?
3. Are the main ideas well supported by adequate elaboration e.g. examples, evidence, illustrations, images etc?
4. Do you have questions or confusion about any ideas that the writer was trying to express? If yes, what are they? Indicate each of them.
5. What are the effective and ineffective parts and why?

Now, *read the paper again very carefully and in detail.* As you read, answer specific questions on the following aspects and identify the problems and suggest improvements.

Content
6. Did the writer adequately explain his/her understanding and reflection, in parts and as a whole? What would you suggest to include for better effectiveness?
7. Were the main and supporting ideas clear? If not, how could the writer clarify?
8. Were the details sufficient and relevant? Indicate those which were inadequate and/or irrelevant.

Organization
9. Were the ideas presented in a logical order and clearly developed throughout the writing?
10. Did the writer use a **thesis statement** and **topic sentences** for organizing the text?
11. Were the paragraphs cohesive and well structured?
12. Was the introduction effective in engaging readers?
13. Was the conclusion effective in summarizing the key concepts?

Language
14. Was this paper accurate in terms of spelling, punctuation and usage? Indicate the mistakes and suggest improvements.
15. Were the sentences clear and concise?
16. Did the writer demonstrate a variety of sentence structures and a good range of vocabulary?

Presentation
17. Did the paper look professional and presentable in layout and format (e.g. consistent and informative headings and subheadings, adequate white space, integration of text and images)?
18. Did the writer include relevant 'aid' for support, e.g. images and graphics etc?

Return the paper and this form to the writer. Discuss your comments with the writer and clarify or expand on any comments where necessary. Be supportive and constructive!

Communicating Orally or in Writing

16. Focused feedback and reflections to inform learning

Wendy Y. K. LAM, The Hong Kong Institute of Education

Summary
This assessment technique aims to provide students with focused and easily accessible feedback on essay assignments. To enable students to get feedback that is clearly linked to the purpose of the assignment and to the assessment criteria, a 'user-friendly' feedback form is designed to inform students of the specific areas where improvements are needed in a draft. In addition, to encourage students to think through the feedback carefully and to take responsibility for their learning, they are required to hand in reflections (attached to the final version of the essay) which highlight specific comments given by the tutor and which they have acted upon to improve their work before submission.

Situations where this practice could be used
This practice could be applied to any kind of written assignment in any discipline.

Background	Focused feedback on a draft forms part of a series of procedures which support the development of an individual essay assignment for first-year students in a Bachelor of Education (Languages) programme.
Rationale	Focused feedback explicitly related to assessment criteria and presented in an easily accessible format provides students with clear directions for improvement in a 'user-friendly' way. Students' written responses to the feedback provide an avenue for them to reflect and act on the tutor's feedback.
Procedure	1. Students submit a draft essay.
	2. The tutor reads through the draft and ticks the appropriate boxes on an Essay Feedback Form. The tutor also writes comments to indicate both the strengths and weaknesses of the draft.
	3. Students get back the draft together with the completed feedback form.
	4. During individual consultations, students raise questions and discuss issues related to the feedback.
	5. After the consultations, students submit the final work together with their response to the feedback (in one short paragraph), highlighting areas that have been improved.
	6. The tutor notes the reflections and grades the essay in the normal way.

Communicating Orally or in Writing

Supporting materials		Essay Feedback Form (Appendix)

Outcomes worth noting	□	Focused feedback indicating students' level of performance effectively draws students' attention to specific areas for improvements. The suggested format also facilitates students' understanding of the feedback.
	□	Students' written reflections show evidence that they have carefully thought through the tutor's feedback and acted upon it.

Student response	□	"The feedback is helpful because it pushes me to make more effort on the part which needs improvement. What's more important, it triggers my thinking about the concepts introduced in the module."
	□	"I think I learnt how to evaluate an essay … The knowledge of how to evaluate an essay will help me to write better essays in my future study."
	□	"The written feedback is helpful to a certain extent. But actually I prefer face-to-face consultations as they can confirm some of my thinking and give me more guidance for improvement."
	□	"It's rather a waste of time writing reflections on the tutor's comments. It's a bit unnatural. Maybe we should spend time improving the draft instead."

How this practice supports learning	• Timely feedback on the draft can be used to improve the final version. The reflective component encourages students to use the feedback in this way.
	• The feedback structure draws students' attention to the assignment criteria, which in turn helps them to internalize these as the basis for evaluating their own work.
	• The requirement for students to indicate on their final assignment how they have used tutor comments pushes them both to act on feedback and explicitly demonstrate that they have done so.

Further suggestions	• Individual consultations could be replaced by a class meeting in which feedback on common errors and suggestions that apply to a number of drafts can be presented and discussed with the class. Students who then want to confer with their tutor individually can do so via email or in a short meeting.
	• Generic feedback can be placed on a course web site.
	• Students could work in pairs to provide feedback to each other, using the Essay Feedback Form, before submitting their draft to the tutor.

Contributor
Wendy Y. K. LAM
The Hong Kong Institute of Education
Email: wlam@ied.edu.hk

APPENDIX

Essay Feedback Form

Student name: _____

Programme: _____

Module: _____

	Great job!	Satisfactory	Work harder!
1. Organization			
2. Degree to which the question is answered			
3. Evidence of reading			
4. Critical thought			
5. Writing style			
6. Internal referencing and reference list			

Overall comments:

Strengths:

Areas for improvement:

Communicating Orally or in Writing

17. Language assessment using an Internet-based discussion board

David ROSSITER and Gibson LAM, The Hong Kong University of Science and Technology

Summary

In this assessment practice, English language students engage in group discussions using an Internet-based communication tool called Gong. Students leave their work on a voice message board, with different topics being covered every week. They receive feedback from their teacher via the same message board, focusing on the students' language skills.

Situations where this practice could be used

This practice is particularly relevant to language learning and other subjects where oral communication is a key skill.

Background	The language assessment described here is conducted in undergraduate English courses. There are approximately 700 students, mostly first year. One face-to-face class and one Internet discussion are held every week.
Rationale	In traditional foreign language classes, students usually do not have enough time to practise their speaking and to receive feedback on this. Moreover, speaking in a large class can be intimidating for many students. The Gong Internet discussion board allows students to speak the language in their own time and place. The students then receive feedback on various aspects of their speaking, such as pronunciation and intonation, through the discussion board in the form of voice and/or text. The text may be written in the student's native language.
Procedure	1. Students form two- or three-person discussion groups in the first week of the course.
	2. A discussion topic with guidelines is set by the teacher every week. For example, students may be instructed to discuss the subject of the World Trade Organization (WTO), with particular focus on the benefits and drawbacks of the organization as it applies to their home country.
	3. Students can prepare their work in groups or individually. They need to leave a fifteen-minute voice discussion in the group message board. Students are encouraged to write some text which is complementary to their audio input. This text is submitted together with the audio recording.
	4. Teachers read and listen to messages and discussions on the board and give feedback primarily on the pronunciation, syntax and phrasing of the student's message.

Communicating Orally or in Writing

5. Further discussion takes place on the discussion board between the students and the teacher. For example, the student will reply to the teacher's feedback, and the teacher will reply to the student. There may be several iterations of this process. A grade is assigned by the teacher at the end of the week according to the linguistic accuracy of the student's input for that week. As a typical semester is comprised of fourteen weeks there will be fourteen such grades for the whole semester.

Supporting materials	The Gong System [http://www.cs.ust.hk/gong]. The most recent version of this can be obtained by emailing the contributors.

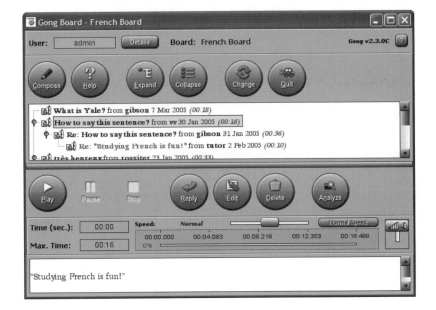

Outcomes worth noting	☐ Improved spoken and written language proficiency. ☐ Flexibility in when and where to engage in the language learning tasks.
Student response	☐ "A very good system which forces us to improve ourselves out-of-class." ☐ "It makes me learn more about how to speak. After this unit, I realized my pronunciation problem." ☐ "The content is somewhat interesting, but it is too troublesome for us to record the discussion through computer." ☐ "I think it uses too much time to record the oral by using Gong."

Communicating Orally or in Writing

How this practice supports learning	• This process requires students to use spoken English on a regular, frequent basis. • By working in small groups, students are able to give and receive feedback from their peers. • Students receive frequent, timely feedback from their teachers which they can apply in their subsequent spoken work.

Further suggestions	• At the end of the course students could be invited to review their progress by listening to the work they submitted over the semester. • Assessment could be by submission of an audio tape or digital recording of oral performances produced in response to feedback. • The discussion board can be part of an integrated online course, including exemplar discussions and guides to various aspects of language.

Contributors

David ROSSITER and Gibson LAM
The Hong Kong University of Science and Technology
Email: rossiter@cs.ust.hk; ibson@cs.ust.hk

▌ Working in Teams ▌

18. Project-based assessment: Designing a web site

Mike KEPPELL, The Hong Kong Institute of Education and David CARLESS, The University of Hong Kong

Summary
This technique seeks to engage students actively through an authentic task, namely the design of a web site for educational purposes. Through this project, students are involved in peer learning, collaborative decision-making and problem-solving. The role of the lecturer is to provide relevant input, act as a 'cognitive coach' or mentor and provide feedback during the process of the assignment.

Situations where this practice could be used
This practice could be applied to any assessment based on a group project.

Background	This assessment task forms part of a module on the topic of multimedia and web authoring. The module is taught through blended learning, a combination of face-to-face teaching and online learning. Students carry out a project assignment in groups of three to five, creating a web site that could be used for their own future teaching in secondary schools. The web site includes a rationale, concept map, educational resources for students, graphics, video, audio and animation.
Rationale	The choice of assessment task is guided by the following principles: ☐ There should be a relationship between the assessment and a real-world task (designing a web site). ☐ Assessment can be co-operative in that students should work in teams. ☐ There can be some element of student choice in the assessment task (i.e. what kind of web site to design) so as to facilitate student engagement and motivation. ☐ The assignment should provide opportunities for tutor feedback on work in progress.
Procedure	1. Input is provided which gives students exposure to design, development and evaluation of multimedia and web technology. 2. Students carry out relevant background readings and share views on them in the online environment. 3. Students form small groups to work on their projects in class, online and outside of class time.

Working in Teams

4. The lecturer provides verbal feedback on work in progress and highlights key issues during class sessions.

5. One week before the submission of the project, each group presents their draft web site design in class.

6. Verbal feedback is again provided to allow groups to refine their web site before final submission.

Supporting materials	☐	Web development software (e.g. Dreamweaver).

Outcomes worth noting	☐	The majority of students find the peer learning processes beneficial.
	☐	Some outstanding work is produced, whilst some groups flounder a little.
	☐	Most students express a positive view of project-based learning, whilst some have negative views.

Student response	☐	"During the process of doing the project, we have to exchange ideas with other group members and we have to find all the project materials and make analysis for it. It helps us to improve communication skills and have deeper thinking."
	☐	"I learn how to discuss with others so as to improve my communication skills."
	☐	"The workload was rather heavy."

How this practice supports learning	• A complex project such as this can require students to work towards a number of required learning outcomes in a module.
	• Such projects typically require a significant amount of work, spread across a semester.
	• Students are required to engage in a range of learning processes including reading, discussion, collaboration, applying skills, and giving and receiving feedback.
	• The process of refining the content of the web site so that it communicates effectively with the intended target audience allows students to deepen significantly their own understanding of the content chosen.
	• Making work public through class presentation often inspires students to do their best work. It also allows students to develop a sense of appropriate standards for their own work by comparing it to the work of their peers.
	• Feedback is provided in time for revisions.

Further suggestions	• Students could be involved in developing criteria for evaluating their own and their peers' draft web sites.
	• Exemplar sites from previous cohorts could be critiqued in order to clarify expectations.
	• A panel drawn from previous cohorts could give feedback on the web sites, perhaps in the context of a prize competition. This need not be associated with the marks or grades awarded by tutors, so that the competition would effectively be a source of further feedback, e.g. on behalf of potential users of these kinds of web sites.
	• Peer feedback could be included as part of the in-class presentations to heighten students' awareness of criteria and standards that they should be applying to their own work.
	• Many aspects of this practice could be conducted online. For example, the final web sites could be placed online for all students to see.

Contributors

Mike KEPPELL[1] and David CARLESS[2]
[1]The Hong Kong Institute of Education; [2]The University of Hong Kong
Email: keppell@ied.edu.hk; dcarless@hkucc.hku.hk

Working in Teams

19. Assessing interpersonal effectiveness in group tutorials

Philip S. L. BEH, The University of Hong Kong

Summary

This practice attempts to address the subjective nature of the assessment of interpersonal effectiveness in group tutorials. Interpersonal effectiveness in team work is a nebulous concept that involves multi-dimensional skills. By outlining some of the skills, such as making suggestions assertively without creating tension, and by involving students themselves in the assessment process, a more objective assessment of student performance is possible. More importantly, students learn from each other's feedback and improve their own interpersonal effectiveness, which ultimately should lead to better performance in group tutorials.

Situations where this practice could be used

- This practice has direct relevance to training professionals who will work in teams directly with patients, clients, customers and colleagues.
- This practice could be adapted to any discipline where assessment of interpersonal effectiveness is not a one-off occurrence, but occurs at regular intervals throughout a semester or year. It is also suitable for assessment that focuses on all aspects of a student's input and participation in the learning process and not just the learning outcomes.

Background	First- to third-year medical students are required to achieve a satisfactory performance in their PBL (problem-based learning) tutorials. Performance in a PBL tutorial involves multifaceted skills, and interpersonal effectiveness is only one of these skills. Students are placed in different groupings and are tutored by at least ten different teachers. Each teacher spends at least eight PBL tutorials with a group of students and is required to assess and share his or her assessment results with the students.
Rationale	This practice seeks to □ promote team work, communication skills and critical analysis; □ enhance objectivity of assessment by involving students as assessors (for feedback initially and possibly grading at a later stage); and □ enhance objectivity of assessment by discussing exemplars or model performances where the assessment criteria are clearly met.
Procedure	1. The stated attributes of 'good' PBL performance in tutorials are presented to all students at the beginning of their entrance into medical school. Examples of performance expected from students include: (a) comparing or contrasting different information and resolving the conflicts if possible; (b) pointing out errors or disagreements in information presented by others, but in an acceptable manner; (c) willingness to compromise for a group consensus.

2. Teachers are also trained and constantly reminded of the meaning of each of the attributes that they should be looking for in student performance.
3. In the first semester of the first year, teachers meet regularly with each student to discuss their good points and provide advice on areas for improvement. Students are also encouraged to discuss their worries, concerns, anxieties, etc.
4. Where necessary, additional teachers may be invited to sit in during tutorials to independently assess and to compare notes.
5. Students are also required to give feedback to and discuss it with each other, in different pairs in each tutorial. Students are told that their peer feedback will often add additional perspectives and insight to the evaluation of the teacher and their feedback performance is monitored by the teacher(s).

Supporting materials	☐ A variety of evaluation forms are in used in different PBL schools and curricula. Forms should be tailored to the needs and stated aims of the particular PBL programme.
Outcomes worth noting	☐ In some of the groups, the team dynamics work so well that students develop separation anxieties when the groups are changed. Lifelong relationships and friendships are built from such groupings.
	☐ When used consistently and regularly, the progress of students can be monitored. This is particularly useful for students who find difficulty adapting to the PBL process.
Student response	Although this process is seen as very important by teachers, students often find it challenging:
	☐ "Teachers may have different expectations and interpretations of what constitutes a satisfactory or outstanding performance."
	☐ "I do not like to evaluate my peers; neither do I like them to evaluate me."
How this practice supports learning	• Problem-based learning is a process which emphasizes student-generated learning and discovery. It also requires good communication skills and good group dynamics. All these qualities are pivotal to promoting more student-centred learning. Evaluation of PBL performance should therefore focus on all aspects of a student's input and participation in the learning.
	• Pro formas and other materials help students to become familiar with important group processes, aspects of their own behaviour that are important in group functioning, and the standards that are expected in this area of their learning.

Working in Teams

	• Students learn a great deal about how their own studies are progressing by the comparisons they are able to make with their fellow students during the various processes of PBL. They are able to make adjustments to improve their own learning accordingly, and learn from each other's strengths and weaknesses.

| **Further suggestions** | • Detailed descriptions of assessment criteria and examples of required attributes are often not sufficient for preparing students for performance or for giving useful peer feedback. Students may need to see and discuss 'model' performances. Sometimes teachers can model them. Another option is to videotape performances by more advanced students and select those that could serve as 'models'.
• Ask students to check ☑ the boxes where clear evidence has been seen of this behaviour, cross ☒ any boxes where negative behaviour has been observed, and leave blank all the boxes where there is insufficient evidence either way.
• 'Shades of grey' could be included, for example having choices such as 'clearly evidenced', 'sometimes evidenced' and 'not noticed' for individual behaviours.
• No peer grading is involved at the initial stage, so that a trusting and collaborative learning atmosphere can be established. Peer grading could be introduced when both teacher and students are comfortable that it would lead to better performance and more varied and objective assessment. |

Contributor
Philip S. L. BEH
Faculty of Medicine
The University of Hong Kong
Email: philipbeh@pathology.hku

Working in Teams

20. Identifying students' misconceptions through peer-assessed presentations

Doris Pui Wah CHENG, The Hong Kong Institute of Education

Summary

When beginning to study a new topic, students in small groups research concepts within that topic and present their findings to the class. This process helps students to recapture their personal knowledge on a specific topic by making it 'public' and allowing scrutiny of this knowledge by means of peer assessment, and enables teachers to access learners' prior knowledge. The tutor is therefore better able to engage with students' understanding and challenge it when necessary as he/she helps students to further construct their own knowledge.

Situations where this practice could be used

This technique, or variations of it, could be used in any situation when students are embarking on a new topic.

Background	This practice has been used with students and teachers in early childhood studies in a teacher education context.
Rationale	Teaching risks becoming spoon-feeding if what is taught does not engage with what is already in students' minds, that is, with their current understanding. Teaching that cannot connect with that understanding tends to be teacher-centred. By providing opportunities for students to make presentations on their existing knowledge at the start of a topic, and to assess each other's presentations, students are able to assess their understanding. Perhaps more importantly, teachers can use their knowledge of students' existing levels of understanding as the basis of further teaching.
Procedure	1. The teacher selects some concepts which students are expected to know before they study a new topic.
	2. Students work in teams to gather information on these concepts from a library or elsewhere.
	3. Each group then presents its information to the whole class in a fifteen to twenty-minute presentation.
	4. While one group is presenting, the other groups assess their performance.
	5. Each group chooses the presentation, apart from their own, which they think is the most impressive, and gives reasons for their choice. They also give feedback to the other groups on how their presentations could be improved.

Working in Teams

6. The teacher then summarizes the feedback and identifies students' misconceptions as and when necessary. The teacher can then pose further questions for student inquiry.

Supporting materials	None required.
Outcomes worth noting	☐ This practice helps students to articulate their personal knowledge through the presentations as well as through their assessment of others' work.
	☐ Students begin to adjust and extend their personal knowledge through the collaborative group discussions and presentations.
	☐ Teachers identify the nature and level of the students' understandings as well as misconceptions of the prerequisite knowledge of a topic and can adapt and adjust their teaching accordingly.
Student response	☐ "We like this way because teaching is not just sitting down and listening to lecturing through PowerPoint."
	☐ "That is our (existing) belief and we didn't know that it (was) problematic" (when students' presentation was being challenged).
	☐ "Our brains are drained and it is very time-consuming."
How this practice supports learning	• Students' prior knowledge when they embark on a new topic often includes deeply embedded misunderstandings. These need to be identified and addressed if new learning is to be effective. This procedure provides a way of getting students to articulate their misunderstandings, as well as providing two sources of immediate challenge to these — their peers and their teacher.
	• Students learn much more through making judgements on what fellow students are presenting than if they were merely listening to their presentations.
	• This 'diagnostic' assessment also provides the basis for ongoing teaching and learning in the topic. Students' new learning builds on what they already know, and teachers can plan their teaching to meet students' needs, while avoiding wasting time on things which the students already know well enough.
Further suggestions	• A simplified version of this practice could be conducted entirely within class time. Students still work in small groups, but use only their existing knowledge without referring to other sources. Alternatively, they could use sources that are readily accessible within the class, including textbooks or reliable Internet sources.

- Students could be asked to self-assess their level of understanding before giving their presentations, and then reassess it afterwards, and reflect on what they had learned from feedback from peers and the teacher.
- Shorter presentations are sometimes as effective as longer ones — brevity demands focus and discipline. Group presentations can be shortened to a few minutes to fit into the class time available.
- Presentations can be placed on a course web site to enable review out of class time.

Contributor

Doris Pui-wah CHENG
School of Early Childhood Education
The Hong Kong Institute of Education
Email: doris@ied.edu.hk

21. Assessing creative team work using ongoing peer critique

Ada Wai Wing MA, The Hong Kong Institute of Education

Summary

This practice utilizes computer-supported team work to create opportunities for and experiences of social creativity. Activities are aligned to an appropriate assessment design to promote working in teams and to foster creativity among learners. The online design allows space for bringing different points of view and resources together to create design communities in which social debate and critique, discussion and reflection, and collaborative knowledge construction can lead to new insights, ideas, and artifacts.

Situations where this practice could be used

This practice of computer-supported collaborative learning can be used in any situation where students are required to work in teams to produce a joint outcome. Tasks need to require genuine collaboration to motivate participation, and require students to plan, prepare drafts for critique, and discuss issues at least partly within a web-based environment.

Background	This practice has been used in a third-year fashion design module in teacher education.
Rationale	This practice is designed to □ model creative teaching and learning in teams; □ fill a gap in assessment regarding the development of creativity; and □ foster creativity online. Online platforms are particularly able to promote creativity in three ways: (a) by publishing creative ideas in different formats, (b) by encouraging follow-up of creative ideas and (c) by evaluating and rewarding creative ideas quickly.
Procedure	1. Students are assigned to a design project with the assessment tasks being integrated into the collaborative activities which involve the use of peer sharing and critique of the group work using the Blackboard Learning Management System. 2. Students conduct weekly intra-group reflections on their design processes to ensure individual accountability, facilitate group processes and make group dynamics transparent. 3. Developmental sketches of design works are posted on the module web site for ongoing feedback and critique from peers and lecturers whenever appropriate. 4. Discussion forums are created and transformed to a learning community that mediates all stages of the process of inquiry in which learners explicate their design concepts, refine their design sketches, and make their ideas publicly open for examination by peers.

Working in Teams

5. Learners are also required to perform an inter-group assessment on the final selected piece of design work by giving feedback to the presenter. It is believed that the learners' social skills, creativity, collaboration, and critical reflective ability are promoted by social interaction and social support in terms of cognitive diversity and distribution of expertise.

Supporting materials	An online learning management system (such as Blackboard or WebCT) that supports the required procedure.
Outcomes worth noting	☐ Students have expressed very positive comments on the design of the collaboration and assessment tasks.
	☐ Creating assessment rubrics, writing intra-group reflective journals, and conducting inter-group peer review have motivated students to take a more active learning role and helped them develop a sense of ownership.
	☐ Students have indicated that working in teams fosters their creativity and cultivates their positive attitude towards collaboration and sharing.
	☐ Learners' openness to feedback is encouraging. The peer feedback is specific and predominantly non-judgmental in tone and form, and directed towards the goals of the recipients. Such useful feedback engages learners in a greater level and depth of reflection, creates intrinsic motivation for improvement and fosters creativity, which is shown in the richer details of the second draft.
Student response	☐ "The assessment rubrics were (developed in) our group discussion. We had learnt a lot from this process as it provided guidelines and directions for our assignment to work on. It also created incentives for our own learning."
	☐ "I think the intra-group reflective journal can help us identify our strengths and weaknesses for improved courses of action. It also acts as a tool for self-reflection and striving for self-enhancement."
	☐ "We can look at other groups' work with the inter-group peer assessment that provides chances for us to experience how a teacher gives marks and constructive comments."
	☐ "Ongoing peer critique makes us review our design work from time to time. As a result, our final version looks very different from our first draft. The improvement is really remarkable!"
How this practice supports learning	• This practice engages students with key issues in a subject over a period of time.
	• It requires engagement at the level of ideas, through online discussion, and with their application as they apply those ideas to a design project.

Working in Teams

- Extensive feedback is provided both within groups and between groups, with the Blackboard environment facilitating ready sharing of work as it develops.
- The continuous flow of feedback allows it to be taken on board all the way through the design process, rather than in one instalment at the end of the process.
- Students are continuously alerted to the qualities of their peers' design work, allowing them to progressively emulate others' excellence, and avoid any pitfalls they observe in their peers' work.
- The process of giving feedback to other groups requires careful consideration of appropriate criteria and helps students develop their ability to gauge the quality of their own work.

Further suggestions	<ul><li>Online learning with multiple groups can be very time-consuming for lecturers. Two steps might make the time required more manageable:<ul><li>– Lecturers might limit their comments to final drafts, with students providing peer feedback on preliminary work. Alternatively, lecturers could have their own comments limited to one brief comment on an intermediate design for each student or group, so that any important redirection is enabled, should students be heading in problematic directions in their work.</li><li>– Following initial modelling and support, students can be encouraged to manage their own online discussions.</li></ul></li><li>Part of the overall assessment could be linked to the quality of students' feedback to each other and their participation in the online discussions. This would encourage all students to be active in the discussions.</li><li>Students could be involved in formulating at least some of the criteria for the assessment of their designs. This would give them a stronger sense of ownership of these assessment criteria, and they would strive more earnestly to achieve them. Furthermore, this exercise would help them to discover which of their own assessment criteria actually 'worked' in practice, and allow them to learn more about the choice of suitable criteria.</li></ul>

Working in Teams

Contributor

Ada Wai Wing MA
Department of Mathematics, Science, Social Sciences and Technology
The Hong Kong Institute of Education
Email: ama@ied.edu.hk

APPENDIX

Assessing Creative Team Work Using Ongoing Peer Critique

Figure 3.1 illustrates how ongoing peer critique can foster creativity in the design process:

SC: *I think your group will give some 'wild' colours and texture to the design, right?*

SG: *Wa! It's so sexy. Which kind of animal has stimulated you to come up with this design? Is it a fox? I think it's quite good in a way that it is ladylike with motion. If the pattern could be drawn in more detail, it would be even better!!! As we are still at the beginning stage, don't give up and let's work harder!*

GA: *Actually the ideas come from ferret and hunter. The lower part of the skirt is made of pieces of ferret feather while the upper part is made of black calfskin. The collar of the black tight-fitting top is made of ferret feather as well. We want to deliver a message of impregnable feeling and the model is taking a role of hunter.*

SP: *It seems that the design will be more balanced if the proportion of the ferret feather is increased.*

First Draft   Second Draft

Figure 3.1   First and second draft of a group of students' fashion design

Working in Teams

▌ **Evaluating Peers** ▌

22. Peer assessment of group projects

Winnie CHENG and Martin WARREN, The Hong Kong Polytechnic University

Summary
This assessment technique involves students in evaluating peers in both the process and the product of learning in group projects. 'Process', which is assessed only by group members, refers to individual students' contributions to the various stages of the group project. 'Product', which is assessed by all other students in the class, refers to the preparation and quality of the various project tasks produced by individual students. Peer assessment forms a part of the overall grade awarded to the group project.

Situations where this practice could be used
This practice could be used in any situation where students work in small groups to produce a product. The procedures it describes are generic.

Background	In an English for Academic Purposes course taught to undergraduate Engineering students, students work in groups on a project comprising three tasks: a seminar, an oral presentation and a report. Each task is assessed by both the class teacher and peers with reference to explicit criteria.
Rationale	Peer assessment can:

Peer assessment can:
- provide learners with the opportunity to take responsibility for analysing, monitoring and evaluating aspects of both the learning process and product of their peers;
- develop students' higher-order reasoning and higher-level cognitive thought;
- nurture student-centred learning;
- encourage active and flexible learning;
- facilitate a deep approach to learning; and
- act as a socializing force and enhance interpersonal relationships within and between groups.

Procedure

1. Prior to the project work, the students receive training in assessing their peers' oral and written assignments against given assessment criteria in order to become familiar with the notion and procedure of peer assessment.

2. At each stage of the group project work, the students are involved in peer assessment.

3. Before and after the assessment process, the students complete questionnaires which aim to find out their attitudes towards peer assessment.

4. Students who show a shift in attitude, whether positive or negative, are identified, and a follow-up interview is carried out.

Supporting materials	☐	This practice is supported by a number of tools, including
		– assessment criteria for the seminar, oral presentation, and written report;
		– an assessment form for group members' contributions to group work;
		– questionnaires on student attitudes towards peer assessment before and after the module; and
		– a student feedback questionnaire on peer assessment of project tasks.
	☐	The seminar assessment criteria and assessment of student contribution form are attached as appendices.
Outcomes worth noting	☐	There has been a positive shift in students' attitudes and confidence as a result of the peer assessment exercise.
	☐	There has been a less positive attitude towards those categories of assessment criteria which were related to assessing the effort or contribution of group members.
	☐	Peer assessment can be usefully and meaningfully employed to factor individual contributions into the grades awarded to students engaged in collaborative group work.
	☐	Agreement in judgement between student and teacher assessments has been found in both language and non-language-related criteria.
Student response	☐	While not entirely comfortable with doing peer assessment in the early stages, students become more comfortable as the exercise progresses.
	☐	Students generally welcome the opportunity to be actively involved in the assessment process.
	☐	Students feel that doing assessment is a means of developing all-round attributes such as social responsibility, leadership and critical thinking.
	☐	Students, on the whole, state that they are fairly and responsibly assessed by their peers.
	☐	Students' attitudes towards different assessment criteria are not uniform. Students are not confident in their ability to judge the appropriateness of writing style and to assess fairly and responsibly their peers' English language.
	☐	Some students are reluctant to judge their fellow group members in relation to the rest of the class.

Evaluating Peers

How this practice supports learning	• This practice includes procedures that are commonly used in peer assessment that are likely to lead to useful outcomes. These include developing the interpersonal skills involved in working closely with fellow students, and developing the ability to critically evaluate the work of others, and hence one's own work. This leads to the critical ability to monitor and improve one's own work while it is being produced.
	• This assessment process reflects the informal or semi-formal ways in which work is often assessed in many fields of professional practice. It therefore provides a useful preparation for students' later work.

Further suggestions	• Class discussion of the peer assessment process could identify students' concerns and highlight what they are learning about the process. In other words, peer assessment itself can be a focus for learning, and developing the capacity to assess others' work, as well as one's own work, becomes a significant learning outcome.
	• Students could be asked to assess their own work using the same criteria as used for peer assessment, and then to reflect on and comment upon any significant differences between the self and peer assessments.
	• Students could be graded on the quality of their marking so as to encourage them to carry out peer assessment seriously.
	• The seminar assessment scale uses the terms 'below average', average' and 'above average'. These are 'normative' terms which involve rating students in comparison with each other. Alternative terms which describe the quality of the student's work, for example 'good' or 'satisfactory' could be used instead.

Contributors

Winnie CHENG and Martin WARREN
The Hong Kong Polytechnic University
Email: egwcheng@polyu.edu.hk; egwarren@polyu.edu.hk

Evaluating Peers

APPENDIX 1

Seminar Assessment Criteria (Class)

Assessing your peers is not an easy task. You need to try to be fair and objective. Your assessment scores will *only* be seen by your teacher. Use the following scale when assessing your fellow students.

1	2	3	4	5
poor	below average	average	above average	excellent

A. Preparation, Overall Presentation and Content of Seminar Paper
   evidence of rehearsal
   consideration of audience
   relevance and interest of material
   quality and appropriacy of visual aids
   well-structured
   clear conclusion(s)

B. Delivery of Seminar Paper
   rapport with and sensitivity to audience
   body language
   timing and pacing
   sensitivity to audience feedback
   use of visual aids
   clarity of delivery
   confidence
   clarity and coordination of group delivery
   satisfactory answers when required
   encouragement of discussion

C. Participating in Seminar Discussion
   relevant questions, comments, ideas
   appropriate academic language

D. Language
   accuracy and appropriate use of
   – vocabulary
   – structures
   – register
   – conciseness
   – clarity of expression

Evaluating Peers

APPENDIX 2

Use the following scale when assessing your fellow students' level of contribution to the group project.

0	1	2	3	4	5
Did not contribute in this way	Poor	Below average	Average	Above average	Excellent

Assessment criteria	Ideas and suggestions for group project	Literature search	Literature analysis	Preparation and planning of seminar presentation	Preparation and planning of oral presentation	Preparation, planning and writing of report	Tota
Group member							

23. Peer assessment of design posters

Ken VOLK, The Hong Kong Institute of Education

Summary
In an information technology course on using graphic design software, student posters are put on display for other students to view and mark using a rubric provided by the teacher. The main aim is for students to develop skills in evaluating quality.

Situations where this practice can be used
This practice can be used for any assignment that uses a display format for students' work. This includes creative and artistic productions, but it can be applied in many disciplines. The widespread use of poster sessions in academic conferences suggests that this format can be used across a broad range of subjects.

Background	This practice has been used with education students studying information technology as part of design and technology modules.
Rationale	This practice is designed to □ promote students' ability to critically evaluate their peers' (and hence their own) work; □ encourage group feedback and participation in the learning process; and □ apply greater objectivity to assessment that could be somewhat subjective.
Procedure	1. Students use Photoshop to create a poster to be used in a school classroom. 2. Students are provided with directions and details regarding grading criteria. 3. After the posters are handed in, they are displayed in a hall with ample room in between. Each poster has a clearly marked letter placed in the corner in place of the student's name. 4. A rubric is provided for each class member to evaluate the posters, including their own. This form is designed to maximize confidentiality, efficiency and objectivity. 5. Students mark each poster independently and submit their marking form to the lecturer. The lecturer averages the students' marks and combines this with his or her own mark. The students' averaged mark typically counts for 50% of the total mark. 6. Students receive a grade, along with the lecturer's comments.

Evaluating Peers

Supporting materials	None.
Outcomes worth noting	☐ Generally (and reassuringly), students' marks match those given by the lecturer.
	☐ For this somewhat subjective assignment, the input by others into the marking process is seen to add to its reliability.
Student response	☐ Students comment that this practice allows them to see others' work and be a part of the total assignment process.
	☐ As future teachers, they appreciate the opportunity to learn about grading processes.
	☐ At first, some students indicate they are a bit uneasy, but with the process repeated throughout the semester, they come to know what to expect and comment that they enjoy the experience.
	☐ This process encourages the sharing of student interaction and feelings, as witnessed by lively critiques exchanged during the process.

How this practice supports learning	• This practice requires students to come to grips with the criteria and standards that apply to this kind of work. Their ability to evaluate their own work is enhanced through the experience of evaluating the work of their peers.
	• Making work 'public' often gives students a higher motivation to produce good work than if the work is to be seen only by their tutor.
	• Students may learn different things about their own work from the comments and grades awarded by peers which supplements the feedback from their tutor.
	• Seeing a range of work also gives students varied perspectives on a topic. They can review their own work in light of this, and develop further insights into alternative understandings and approaches.

Further suggestions	• While a wall of posters allows students to easily see and comment on their colleagues' work, posters could also be placed on a course web site for this purpose. This would make them readily accessible and allow them to be viewed again at any time during the course.
	• The self-assessment could be separated from the peer assessment by asking all students to self-assess their posters on a separate sheet. This would allow self and peer assessment to be compared, and it would help identify students who had unreasonable (whether too high or too low) views about the merits of their own particular posters.
	• The poster exhibition could be assessed in parallel by 'visitors' — for example other tutors, or members of the public, or teachers from local

Evaluating Peers

schools. This extra data on assessment could be compared with students' peer assessment data, helping to illustrate how objective the latter process may be.

- Students could be allowed to develop criteria for the peer assessment in advance of preparing the posters, so that they have ownership of the criteria from the outset, and could therefore strive more earnestly to meet the criteria in their work.
- Students and the tutor could simply provide helpful comments and suggestions for improvement at this stage, with a revised version submitted for marking.

Contributor

Ken VOLK
Department of Information and Applied Technology
The Hong Kong Institute of Education
Email: kvolk@ied.edu.hk

Evaluating Peers

24. Training students to peer and self-evaluate their writing

Nigel BRUCE, The University of Hong Kong

Summary
Over three four-week cycles, first-year undergraduates are taught how to apply a set of criteria of effective writing to their own and their classmates' assignments. The aim is that they become more autonomous in shaping and improving their own writing.

Situations where this practice could be used
This technique can be applied to student writing in any discipline.

Background	This technique relates to a course teaching legal problem answer writing for first-year law students. The approach places a strong emphasis on training students to take on the evaluative work of the teachers as a means of making them more autonomous in improving their academic and professional writing (see Bruce, 2002, for a fuller account).
Rationale	The aim is that students become more autonomous in shaping and improving their own writing, once the support of the English teacher has been removed. Through a recycling of a revision-based written assignment, they are taught how to take ownership of the means by which their writing will typically be judged by their teachers and future employers.
Procedure	1. Each of three assignments is taken through a four-week cycle (see table), with the teaching and feedback focus moving from content to language, via attention to argumentation and organization. Students apply an ongoing revision process, applying criteria for effective realization of these core objectives at each stage, as set out in the attached peer evaluation matrix.
	2. Weeks 1/2. Students analyse an assignment — in this case, writing a solution to a legal problem — and then write their first draft, focusing on content issues.
	3. Weeks 2/3. Students review their first draft in pairs, applying 'content' criteria; then each pair feeds back to the whole class; the tutor then works through argumentation tasks, and assigns the first revision, focusing on those criteria.
	4. Weeks 3/4. Students review their second draft in pairs, applying content and argumentation criteria, with feedback to the whole class; the tutor then works through organization and language issues and criteria, and assigns a second revision, focusing on these criteria.
	5. Weeks 3/4. Students review their third and final draft, applying the full set of criteria (see appendix); after feedback, the tutor may choose

to work through a 'model' text or extract to illustrate the target standard for the students.

6. This revision cycle can be illustrated as follows:

Table 3.1 The revision cycle

Spectrum: *Legal* ⟵——————————————⟶ *Linguistic*

Feedback focus →	A. Content issues	B. Argumentation /Reasoning	Organization/ Structure	Grammar, vocabulary
My legal writing example	Legal analytical skills and content	Legal argumentation 'moves'[1]	Possibly recycling B, with variations	Legal expressions and terminology
Progression	Weeks 1/2	Weeks 2/3	Weeks 3/4	

Issue → Principle + Case precedent → Application → Conclusion

Supporting materials	☐ Peer evaluation matrix — general (attached) ☐ Peer evaluation criteria — applied to legal writing (attached) ☐ Web site: http://ec.hku.hk/law
Outcomes worth noting	By the end of one semester, students are more comfortable talking about writing and discussing what makes their writing effective. This is a behaviour, though, that requires training over a whole semester, as a whole meta-discourse needs to be learnt, and a number of taboos — about expert judgements, face loss — need to be overcome.
Student response	☐ Most students agree they have improved their own writing by having been placed in a peer-evaluating position. ☐ Some students remain unconvinced that they can improve their own writing by the practice of reviewing and critiquing their classmates' writing; on reflection the recycling approach requires more variety of writing tasks, perhaps assigning more focused and varied critiquing tasks.
How this practice supports learning	• This practice focuses on helping students develop the capacity to monitor the communicative quality of their own work while they are in the process of writing it. This capacity depends on their understanding the criteria and standards that will be used by teachers to evaluate their work. • Students have the opportunity to emulate good practice that they observe in the work of their peers, and to avoid pitfalls which they notice in other students' work.

Evaluating Peers

- Students find out more about the nature of the criteria which tutors will use to judge the quality of their writing, and progressively can work towards demonstrating their achievement accordingly.
- Students are alerted to the balance between 'content' criteria and 'structure' criteria in their work.
- The provision of criteria and explicit standards for each criteria allows both students and tutors to engage with the foundation of good evaluation.

Further suggestions	• Students could be involved in formulating at least some of the criteria by which their writing would be assessed, so that they have a greater sense of ownership of the criteria as a whole. • Common problems identified by the students could be the focus of class discussion. • Common problems in writing could be noted on the course web site, with suggestions for addressing them. • Students could be given feedback from tutors on how well (or otherwise) they applied the criteria to their peers' work so that students understanding of the criteria could be continuously developed.

Reference
Bruce, N. (2002) Dovetailing language and content: Teaching balanced argument in legal problem answer writing. *English for Specific Purposes*, 21, 4, 321–45.

Csontributor
Nigel BRUCE
The English Centre
The University of Hong Kong
Email: njbruce@hku.hk

Peer Evaluation Matrix for an Academic Writing Course: Broad Criteria only Listed
[see over for completed set of target criteria for each grade]

Circle the grade you think the script deserves for each of the four-skill criteria, and add comments in the boxes

Aspect		Legal Content Problem Analysis	Legal Reasoning/ Argumentation	Organization of the whole answer	Language
Criteria		A. **Knowing** the content; **analysing** the assignment/problem for the appropriate substantive answer	B. **Realizing** the relevant reasoning or argumentative 'moves' in an appropriate sequence	C. **Structuring and balancing** the argument to fit the expectations of the genre	D. **Articulating** clearly, via grammar — connectors, tenses, modals — and vocabulary
Grade					
A	A	1st draft: students are asked to write — and then peer-evaluate — applying the criteria in A, broadly summarized above, but illustrated in detail in tasks covered before or after the 1st draft. In the 1st of the 3 cycles, I prefer to assign this as an <u>in-class</u> writing task, as I use the task to assess students' competency at the task prior to the intervening teaching and learning process.	2nd draft: As in A, but the 1st revision is a take-home task, following intensive task-based teaching of the argumentative or reasoning strategies or routines expected by the discipline in the particular assignment genre targeted. E.g. in research introductions: 1. claim significance for your topic; 2. review current knowledge; 3. indicate a gap; 4. say how you'll fill that gap.	3rd and final draft (2nd revision) — either a take-home or in-class task, depending on scale and difficulty. The tasks here should address language issues (D) at the service of argumentative "moves" (B), with the focus increasingly on editing and proofreading. If this assignment is to count towards the course assessment, students will likely opt to "tidy up" their text prior to submission.	In this approach — dovetailing language and content — there is no separate phase for attending to language issues. With experience, these will be anticipated and woven into the tasks in all phases. Subject teachers should liaise with their language counterparts for advice on which problems to target, and what kinds of tasks will afford the most productive practice.
	A-				
B	B+				
	B				
	B-				
C	C+				
	C				
	C-				
	D+				
D/F					

Other comments:

Evaluating Peers

English for Law: Writing Problem Solutions: Evaluating Problem Answers
Student Peer Evaluation Criteria for Legal Problem Question Answers (PQAs)

Aspect / Criteria Grade	Legal Content and Problem Analysis	Legal Reasoning / Argumentation	Organization of the whole answer	Language: grammar and vocabulary
	Knowing the law: theory, precedent cases and analogous facts; **analysing** the facts and **identifying** what is really at issue	**Applying:** principles to facts, and **Arguing** each party's case via **IPCAC**[1] **reasoning**, involving identifying the issues, and applying relevant legal case precedent for both principle(s) and factual analogy to decide those issues.	**Structuring and balancing** PQAs economically and logically; levels: *Macro:* **Tort:** Duty, Breach etc. *Micro:* IPCAC	**Articulating** clearly, via **Grammar:** conditional connectors, tenses, modals, punctuation; **Vocabulary:** appropriate choice and forms of words, esp. in combination
A	Legal analysis: **complete** grasp of relevant law: what is at issue, and **excellent** in selecting and using appropriate case precedents and analogous facts	Argumentation: **Closely and persuasively** follows reasoning sequence in negligence — both by issues and applying IPCAC	Organization: **Highly efficient** in applying principle to the PQ, works systematically through relevant issues and IPCAC; offers a balanced assessment of chances of recovery	Grammar: full **mastery** of complex sentence structures, tense forms, conditional and concessive structures, and punctuation; Vocabulary: native-like choice and use of vocabulary
B	Legal analysis: **reasonable** grasp of relevant law: what is at issue, and key case precedent support but **moderate** ability to analogize with precedent facts	Argumentation: **Mostly follows** reasoning sequence in negligence — both by issues and applying IPCAC	Organization: **Reasonably competent** in applying principle to PQ, good sequencing of issues and IPCAC; offers some balanced assessment of parties' chances of recovery	Grammar: generally **competent** use of complex sentence structures, tense forms conditional and concessive structures, and punctuation Vocabulary: good level of choice and form
C	Legal analysis: **weak** grasp of relevant law: and what is at issue in the PQ, cases cited routinely and often **inappropriately** and **minimal** application of analogous facts	Argumentation: **Some lapses** in reasoning sequence in negligence — both by issues and applying IPCAC	Organization: **Weak** in applying principle to the PQ, inconsistent sequencing of issues and IPCAC; fairly crude assessment of parties' chances of recovery	Grammar: **weak** use of complex sentence structures, tense forms and modals, and punctuation — these shortcomings may obscure more complex ideas. Vocabulary: frequent problems, occasionally affecting understanding of message
D/F	Legal analysis: **confused** grasp of relevant law: generally unable to identify what is at issue in the PQ, and **weak** ability to apply relevant rules and principles	Argumentation: **Hardly follows** the reasoning sequence in negligence — either by issues or by applying IPCAC	Organization: **very weak and inconsistent** in applying principle to the PQ, very weak sequencing of issues and IPCAC; may omit to assess parties' chances of recovery	Grammar: **avoidance or very weak** use of complex sentences, and control of tenses, modals (conditionals) and punctuation: all obscuring the writer's meaning

1. IPCAC stands for this common law legal reasoning sequence: Issue — Principle + Case precedent — Application (of case) — Conclusion.

Other comments:

25. Technology-facilitated peer assessment of music creation

Rita Lai Chi YIP, The Hong Kong Institute of Education

Summary
The practice is designed to enhance students' ability to assess their own music creation. Students utilize selected computer-based music technology in the creation of their own music. In directing students to do the creative work, criteria for assessment are discussed to ensure that students understand the focus of the music composition. During the process of music creation, students save their work, listen to the drafts, check against the criteria set, and make revisions whenever necessary. Time in class is scheduled for students to play their music with the help of the computer to their peers for verbal feedback. Students can upload their drafts for further online peer assessment or teacher comment.

Situations where this practice could be used
This practice, with its use of specialized software and equipment, is designed for creating, recording and revising musical compositions in the specific context of music education. Similar processes may well apply to aiding creative development in many other areas of performing arts education, particularly when the aural dimension is significant.

Background	This technique has been used in teacher education in music.
Rationale	Music creation as an art of sound in time to convey personal thoughts and feelings may be more easily appraised when the sound is heard. The conventional practice of writing music on paper without much chance of it being performed poses a significant limitation to feedback and learning. With the introduction of relevant computer programmes and a web teaching platform, students' music creation can be charted for self and peer assessment more effectively.
Procedure	1. Students are directed to formulate their thoughts about a new music composition. Attention is drawn towards shaping their music with a range of music elements such as tempo, meter, timbre, dynamics, key, harmony, and formal structure.
	2. A computer-based music software program is introduced to students to help create their music.
	3. Sufficient time is allowed for exploration and experimentation of music ideas, and then developing them with various possibilities provided by the music program.
	4. Criteria of assessment regarding originality, fluency, flexibility, elaboration and expressiveness of their music are discussed with students to ensure they understand how to assess their own music creation.

Evaluating Peers

5. Time in class is scheduled for students to play their music, with the help of the computer, to their peers for verbal feedback.

6. Students have the option of uploading their drafts to the Blackboard web teaching platform for written comment from peers and/or the teacher.

7. Upon receiving feedback, students can continue to revise their work. They are encouraged to consult with the teacher about any questions.

8. At the end of their music creation, students write a reflection on their creative process in addition to accounting for their work concisely. This allows another opportunity for students to review their music composition — in effect to assess their own work — and make final modifications before submission.

Supporting materials	☐	Computer programs for music creation (e.g., sequencing programs such as *Sonar* or *Cubase*; notation programs such as *Finale* or *Sibelius*) and/or a MIDI piano keyboard which can be connected to the computer.
Outcomes worth noting	☐	The music and notation created by students are captured more easily. This provides a comparatively concrete means for the teacher, when assessing their music composition, to communicate with students regarding their perception of the theoretical and aesthetic aspects of the music they have created.
	☐	The development of students' inner hearing of music, the ability to perceive sound through sight, is facilitated.
	☐	Students are more cautious about what to listen for in assessing their peers' and their own work according to the criteria.
	☐	It is easier to chart the progress of students' work for formative as well as summative assessment.
Student response	☐	"I can listen more objectively to my music and make revisions instantly."
	☐	"The music can be recorded and performed more exactly as I intended. It can also be played back for comment by peers and others. I then knew what they like or dislike about my music and modified it based on those comments."
	☐	"Revisions made to the music could be played to hear how effective the changes are. This helped me to further improve my work."
	☐	"I begin to like creating music more because I can control the sound. I can show others more easily how I structured my music."
	☐	"To have my work uploaded for open criticism made me feel a bit uneasy."

Evaluating Peers

How this practice supports learning	• This practice combines the use of explicit criteria with peer and self assessment processes. Being able to listen to one's composition is a powerful form of feedback in itself.
	• The public nature of this peer feedback is likely to encourage students to produce good work. It also allows them to see and hear their peers' work, thereby accessing other possible approaches that they might take, and avoiding in their own creations things they find they do not like about peers' work.
	• The requirement to reflect on the creative process may heighten students' awareness of their responses to feedback from others and may help them in developing the capacity to evaluate the quality of their own work while they are producing it.
	• The need to revise work after feedback ensures that students will take notice of the feedback. The in-class feedback also becomes a valuable basis for classroom discussion.
	• The discussion of criteria, rather than merely presenting criteria to students, provides an opportunity for students to come to grips with them and to work out exactly what they may mean in the context of their own creative work.

Further suggestions	• Students could be asked to identify and prioritize the criteria which they believe should relate to assessing the creativity of their own music compositions. These criteria could then be shared and discussed by the whole group, and an agreed sub-set of the criteria could be identified to apply to all students' future works. This could lead to an increased sense of ownership of the assessment criteria for creative work.
	• An opportunity for students to hear (and see) each others' final compositions may encourage even higher quality work at the final stage of this process. This could take the form of a presentation at the end of the course.
	• After hearing each others' compositions, students could be asked to redefine the criteria which would be most suitable to distinguish between 'excellent' and 'ordinary' examples of musical creativity.

Contributor

Rita Lai Chi YIP

The Hong Kong Institute of Education

Email: lcyip@ied.edu.hk

Evaluating Peers

▮ Learning Autonomously ▮

26. 'Learning-through-assessment': Assessment tasks that challenge more accomplished students

CHAN Hau Ping and MOK Yan Fung, City University of Hong Kong

Summary

In a class of mixed ability students, fundamental concepts are taught fully in class, while higher-level content is noted. Students are encouraged to study the textbook for higher-level content, which is assessed by using a 'bonus' section of a test, with questions structured so that students can actually learn as they address them. Further learning occurs when the bonus questions are discussed.

Situations where this practice could be used

- This practice can be used to encourage students to deal with more difficult content in a subject — it separates basic concepts from higher-level ones and provides an innovative way of assessing the higher-level content. The practice could be used when content in a subject can be distinguished in this way, and when tutors want to encourage more able students to extend themselves.
- The underlying ideas and approach could be adapted to many learning and assessment situations.

Background	This practice evolved from the challenges of teaching and assessing a large class of mixed ability students majoring in Electrical Engineering.
Rationale	☐ 'Learning-through-assessment' requires pre-assessment preparatory learning, learning through guided questions to tackle problems during the time of assessment, and reflecting on one's 'mis-learning' by post-assessment performance analysis. The second aspect requires learning and assessing at the same time. If well designed as a form of discovery learning, it can enhance students' learning and reward those who have prepared well for examinations.
	☐ This learning-through-assessment is particularly suitable for teaching mixed ability students. The approach is to (a) teach all students the fundamentals, (b) touch on some higher-level content and encourage more self-study of this content, and (c) assess and encourage learning of the high-level content through bonus marks in examinations. The average-ability students are taught what is required while the higher-ability students are challenged and allowed to develop their learning to higher levels.

Procedure   ☐   This strategy has three stages: (a) pre-assessment learning of the required knowledge, as well as learning about the assessment format; (b) learning subject knowledge through exercising domain-related thinking skills in tackling unfamiliar problems at the time of assessment; and (c) after assessment, reflecting on one's 'mis-learning' and gaps in learning by analysing one's performance in the assessment. The second aspect, which includes the notion of 'learning-through-assessment', requires questions that can both guide learning and serve the purpose of assessing student ability.

☐   Students' learning and assessment can be improved by integrating the three stages to form a learning loop in which the three stages inform and enhance each other.

Preparation

1. The fundamentals of the subject are fully taught in class, while higher-level content is highlighted but not covered in detail. Students are encouraged to further develop their knowledge of the higher-level content through studying the textbook.

The mid-term test

2. The fundamentals are assessed in mid-term test papers. The higher-level knowledge is assessed in a bonus section.

The bonus section

3. The bonus section is structured to encourage all students to attempt it. It is divided into three questions.

4. In *question 1*, students are guided to use a particular method ('method A') to tackle a problem. All students should be able to tackle this question.

5. In *question 2*, they are induced to develop a tool to evaluate method A. The evaluation tool suggests to the students that there are deficiencies in the method, namely that it is not very accurate, and that they should employ another, more accurate method in tackling the first question. Students who can manage question 2 go on to the third question.

6. *Question 3* requires students to use method B, which is part of the higher-level content not fully taught in class. Students develop this knowledge as they answer questions one and two. Students will discover, by comparing the results of methods A and B, that method B is highly accurate.

7. The bonus questions are a form of guided discovery learning that can help students to learn something of a higher level. This learning begins at the preparation stage when students are encouraged to learn some higher-level content. Without such preparation, the guided learning-at-the-time-of-assessment would not be effective. The bonus questions also serve to distinguish students of different levels and to reward them accordingly.

Learning Autonomously

Post-test discussion

8. Method B is explained in class after the exam. Students are provided with a statistical analysis sheet denoting the scores carried by each question, the highest and lowest scores achieved in the class, the averages and the standard deviations. Students can see the standards they have achieved and reflect on the 'mis-learning' and discovery learning they have undertaken with regard to the learning-through-assessment loop.

Supporting materials	☐ Several examples are used to teach the fundamentals.
	☐ The higher-level part must be well covered and explained in the textbook for students' self-study.
	☐ Statistical analyses of students' performance.
Outcomes worth noting	An analysis of student papers shows that:
	☐ Students who did well on questions one and two either did well or not well on question three. This shows that question three was discriminating between students with different ability levels.
	☐ Students who did not do well on questions one and two might not even have understood the fundamentals well. The third question was clearly a higher-level question that did not fit their current capability.
Student response	Students report that this assessment practice:
	☐ motivates them to think about the more difficult parts of the question;
	☐ encourages them to think more deeply; but
	☐ does not allow enough time to attempt all questions.

How this practice supports learning	• This practice focuses on providing a challenge for more able students by encouraging them to extend their learning beyond what is covered in class, and then assessing this extended learning in a structured set of questions which are themselves designed to promote learning.
	• Less able students are given the opportunity to see the greater depth at which they should eventually be able to learn, but can also concentrate their learning on the fundamental principles first.
	• Learning occurs through a cycle of (a) preparatory reading, (b) attempting to complete the three bonus questions, and (c) the feedback provided by the post-test explanation and discussion.
	• Setting high expectations can motivate students to do their best.

Further suggestions	• The practice could be used in formative tasks as well in tests that count towards a final grade.

Learning Autonomously

- A bank of examples could be built up to demonstrate to future students the varying levels of performance which can be expected from students of different levels of ability or experience.
- A parallel process can be used in other forms of assessment such as projects or essays where higher level or additional requirements for higher grades are clearly specified.

Contributors

CHAN Hau Ping and MOK Yan Fung

City University of Hong Kong

Email: eehpchan@cityu.edu.hk; yfmok3@cityu.edu.hk

27. Using portfolio assessment to promote autonomous learning

MAK Wai Ho, City University of Hong Kong

Summary

Students are required to submit a portfolio of seven types of documents at the end of the semester as evidence of learning. The portfolio aims to foster students' sense of responsibility for their own learning as well as helping them develop effective strategies for independent learning.

Situations where this practice could be used

The portfolio approach described here could be applied to any situation where students are required to submit a number of documents as evidence of their learning.

Background	This practice has been used with students in a full-time associate degree programme in translation and interpretation.
Rationale	The portfolio assessment used has the following objectives: ☐ to raise students' awareness of their own learning behaviour; ☐ to let students understand the importance of their own responsibility in their learning; ☐ to help students develop effective strategies and habits for learning independently; and ☐ to extend students' learning experiences beyond the classroom and textbook reading.
Procedure	At the 10th week (of a 13-week semester) students submit a portfolio, which consists of seven sets of documents, as evidence of their learning. These sets are: 1. a learning plan; 2. concept maps; 3. focused analysis of authentic texts; 4. a review of their progress; 5. sentence imitation; 6. solving grammatical problems; and 7. extra documents. Some of the documents (e.g. 1, 2, 4) are collected and marked earlier so that students will spread their work evenly throughout the semester.
Supporting materials	None.

Learning Autonomously

Outcomes worth noting	☐	The portfolio documents cover important metacognitive and cognitive skills in grammar learning.
	☐	The portfolio is flexible enough to allow students to set their own learning goals and to select activities which interest them personally, which are related to their professional development, or which suit their own learning styles and aspirations.
	☐	Tutors enjoy the opportunity to respond to students' remarks, queries and reflections. The portfolio also offers opportunities for appreciation of students' work, hence reinforcing their positive learning experiences.
	☐	Students submit a great variety of documents, including grammar web sites; vocabulary notebooks; grammar exercises with remarks; critical analyses of texts; questions about grammar; e-mail and letter samples in which students discuss grammar with friends; commentaries on newspaper grammar columns and grammar textbooks; and comments on grammar issues they encounter in their everyday life.
Student response	☐	The end-of-term evaluation questionnaire survey indicates that students particularly enjoy the freedom and flexibility that is part of the portfolio approach.
	☐	Some have remarked that this has been the first time in their life when they have planned their own study. In the past they have only studied what the teacher taught and only done the exercises given by the teacher.
	☐	Some students have said that they had never previously thought of the strengths and weaknesses of their grammar.
	☐	Students' eagerness to share their 'new discoveries' can be felt in the class.

| **How this practice supports learning** | This practice shows several of the benefits of the portfolio approach:
• Students accept more responsibility for their learning, within a clearly structured framework.
• As students reflect on their learning, they become aware of what they know and where their weaknesses lie — they develop the capacity to evaluate their own work.
• The approach allows students to bring experiences from their everyday life into the picture of their academic development of English grammar.
• In following their own interests, students can make some interesting discoveries.
• In creating a diverse portfolio, students are required to meet a range of objectives, and the portfolio requires them to work consistently over the semester. |

Learning Autonomously

Further suggestions	• Students often find it difficult to handle the portfolio approach. Three steps might help them with this:
	– They can be involved in classroom discussion of criteria and standards for good portfolios.
	– They could be given examples of portfolios from previous students to critique.
	– They could be invited, or required, to give feedback to, and seek feedback from fellow students.
	• Students could be asked to include a self-assessment of their own portfolios, against clearly specified criteria, as one of the documents in their portfolios. They could then be given feedback, where necessary, about how effective their self-assessment has been.
	• There is a growing trend towards 'e-portfolios'. Developing portfolios on a course web site enables lecturers and students alike to access work as it develops and when it is completed. The process of making work 'public' in this way also provides incentive to produce higher-quality work.

Contributor

MAK Wai Ho
Division of Language Studies
City University of Hong Kong
Email: lswhmak@cityu.edu.hk

Learning Autonomously

28. Exemplars and assessing independent learning

Ngar-Fun LIU, The Hong Kong Institute of Education

Summary
This assessment technique focuses on getting students to do high quality work independently. Students are induced to do so by exemplars collected from several cohorts of learners and by having to make their own work 'public'. Further encouragement to produce quality work includes the opportunity for receiving feedback for improvement. Grading is delayed to the end of the course, and learners choose two out of the four assignments to be graded.

Situations where this practice could be used
Two core assessment elements can be applied (with relevant modification) in a very wide range of contexts:
- presenting students with models of exemplary work to guide their own assignments (together with criteria, and commentary on the ways in which the models satisfy the criteria);
- providing regular structured feedback to students, from the teacher and student peers, on work in progress.

Any assessment that calls for an open-ended piece of written work or a physical performance from students might profitably include these elements, suitably adapted to the particular context.

Background	This technique has been developed and used in English language courses for Hong Kong university students.

Rationale	☐ Students often have problems in understanding fast speech delivered by non-Hong Kong English speakers in one-way listening situations. Outside class practice and evidence of such practice is required in the form of four listening reports and other shorter assignments. However, the quality of reports is not consistently high and there may be little evidence that skills taught or practised in class are consciously practised or applied. The report format has been revised to reflect the desired learning outcomes, and exemplars and peer feedback have been introduced.
	☐ This assessment practice aims to support:
	– development of effective independent learning through identifying learning aims and problem-solving strategies;
	– application of strategies and skills learned in class; and
	– enhancement of the ability to monitor and reflect on one's own learning through self and peer feedback.

Learning Autonomously

Procedure	1. In class, students look at several model listening reports in groups. Then, each group outlines one section of the report to the whole class.
	2. The teacher uses Appendices 1 (Report Structure) and 2 (Feedback Form) to sum up what is expected of the listening assignment and to answer questions about the assignment. Both appendices serve the purpose of enhancing students' ability to focus and reflect on their own learning.
	3. Outside class, students choose their listening material and set specific practice aims on their own.
	4. They listen to the material and recount their listening practice experience in the form of a practice report.
	5. The report is submitted to the teacher and one other student, who use Appendix 2 to give comments before the next report is due. Generic feedback is given to the whole class by the teacher.
	6. Students are required to keep the reports and feedback forms (teacher's and peers') in a folder, so that they can demonstrate their response to feedback in subsequent reports and see evidence of their own progress (and perhaps gain better grades as a result).
	7. Students submit all reports and feedback forms at the end of the course and choose two out of the four reports to be graded by the teacher.

Supporting materials	☐ Structure of Listening Report (Appendix 1)
	☐ Feedback Form for Listening Report (Appendix 2)
	☐ Model listening reports
	☐ Examples of listening aims and strategies
	☐ List of audio-visual or listening materials, by type and level, on the radio, television and Internet that have recently been used by students

Outcomes worth noting	☐ Students tend to submit high-quality listening reports, possibly because of peer pressure and having studied model reports.
	☐ However, in view of the fact that the listening report and feedback form are initiated by the teacher, students' reactions and perceptions to them should be solicited, formally or informally, after their first or second attempt. This gives the teacher a chance to tackle potential problems early on in the course.
	☐ Student feedback has resulted in changing two of the four written reports into oral reports. The oral reports are presented in the teacher's office in groups of four, with each student given only five minutes to do so.

Student response	☐ "Having looked at and discussed model assignments done by past students, I had a good idea of what is expected."
	☐ Informal feedback from students suggests that some find the well-defined structure of the report too constraining and would rather have more freedom to write whatever they like.

Learning Autonomously

☐   The pressure of making one's work 'public' seems too much at the beginning as some students spend a disproportionate amount of time on the assignment and complain about the heavy workload.

How this practice supports learning	There are many ways in which this approach promotes learning: • The assessment requirements are aligned with the curriculum objectives. • The assessment tasks, (high) expectations, criteria and standards are clearly documented and ongoing course and teaching activities engage students in studying and understanding these. • The assessed tasks engage students in productive learning activity that spreads time and effort evenly across the course. • Students' work is made public — this encourages serious effort from students, enables feedback on work in progress from different sources, and enables students to learn by observing and reflecting on the efforts of their peers. • Feedback is structured so that it is focused on learning criteria and standards. • Students are able to act upon the feedback in order to improve their ongoing work and enhance their learning.

Further suggestions	• Criteria could be the focus of class discussion early in the course to help students clarify expectations. • Towards the end of the course, students could use the Feedback Form as a self-assessment tool prior to submitting their reports. • Exemplars can be collected over time and from a variety of contexts to illustrate that there can be different ways of achieving an outstanding result.

Contributor

Ngar-Fun LIU
The Hong Kong Institute of Education
Email: nfliu@ied.edu.hk

Learning Autonomously

APPENDIX 1

Structure of Listening Report

Please organize your Listening Report using the following sections and limit it to two to three pages. The 'model' listening reports you have looked at in class and this structure should help you plan your listening practice, from choosing the material, setting practice aims, and dealing with listening problems to writing up a report.

Student I.D. Number:	Name of Listening Material/Programme:
Assignment Number:	Type of Listening Material/Programme:
Course Code:	Source (e.g., channel, date, time):

1.   Practice Aims
Why did you choose the listening material and what did you want to achieve in this listening practice?

2.   Problems and Strategies
What problems did you encounter while listening and how did you deal with them?

3.   Self-assessment
To what extent have your practice aims been achieved? What have you learned from dealing with the problems? What improvements (if any) would you make if you were to do the whole assignment again?

4.   Summary of Content
In less than 50 words, describe what the listening material/programme is about.

5.   Response to Content
What did you think of the listening material/programme? Did you enjoy it? Were you upset by it? Your response could be emotional, intellectual or personal.

6.   New words/expressions
Present the words/expressions in the context in which you heard them in the programme, i.e., the words that come *before* and *after* the new expression should be included. What did you think the words/expressions mean in the context? There will be occasions when the utterances are not at all clear to you. However, you could still present them in transliteration, i.e., spell them out as they sound to you.

APPENDIX 2

Feedback Form for Listening Report

Feedback given by (Please tick one box):   ☐ Teacher   ☐ Peer   ☐ Self

Rate each of the following criteria by (a) considering the descriptions at both ends of the 6-point scale and (b) circling a number.

Choice of listening material		
Appropriate for level	6 5 4 3 2 1	Inappropriate for level
Appropriate for aim(s)	6 5 4 3 2 1	Inappropriate for aim(s)
Aim(s)		
Realistic/appropriate	6 5 4 3 2 1	Unrealistic/inappropriate
Creative/varied	6 5 4 3 2 1	Little evidence of creativity
Problem-solving strategies		
Original/creative strategies	6 5 4 3 2 1	Little evidence of creative strategies
Adequate use of strategies	6 5 4 3 2 1	Inadequate use of strategies
Self-assessment		
Consistent with stated aims	6 5 4 3 2 1	Inconsistent with stated aims
New words/expressions learned		
Many examples in context	6 5 4 3 2 1	Few or no examples in context
Response to content of material		
Relate to experience/knowledge	6 5 4 3 2 1	Little or no attempt at relating to experience
Thoughtful/critical	6 5 4 3 2 1	Little evidence of thoughtful response
Language and Presentation		
Correct spelling	6 5 4 3 2 1	Many spelling mistakes
Appropriate use of words	6 5 4 3 2 1	Inappropriate use of words
Few grammatical mistakes	6 5 4 3 2 1	Many grammatical mistakes
Few lengthy/jumbled sentences	6 5 4 3 2 1	Many lengthy/jumbled sentences
Easy-to-read layout	6 5 4 3 2 1	Difficult-to-read layout

Please comment on **one** area for improvement:

_____

_____

_____

Learning Autonomously

29. Formative assessment of projects in progress

Louisa LAM, The Hong Kong Institute of Education

Summary
Students working on independent projects are given support at each stage of the project. This support includes meetings with an advisor (staff member), talks from experts in specific project areas, and receiving feedback on presentations from lecturers and peers.

Situations where this practice could be used
This could be a useful practice in situations where students undertake a project of their own choosing. The process of inviting outside experts to meet with students who are pursuing similar topics, and the use of presentations and peer feedback to improve the projects, could be applied in many disciplines.

Background	This technique is used with students studying mathematics in a pre-service education degree programme.

Rationale

Students often find independent project work both particularly challenging and uniquely satisfying. This practice supports project work by:

- providing advice and feedback to students as they work independently on projects;
- providing assistance in areas that would be beneficial to students; and
- establishing channels for improving students' project work in the following year by reviewing project outcomes and suggesting modifications to the process.

Procedure

At the project proposal stage

1. The student's project proposal is considered by the module coordinator, and an advisor with relevant expertise is assigned.
2. The advisor (a staff member) meets with the student to sharpen and develop the proposal in a fuller form.
3. From the proposals, areas of interest common to most students are identified and talks by experts in these areas are arranged. These talks allow for questions and discussion with the experts.

Conducting the project

4. The student has discussions with his or her advisor over the several months of the project.
5. About a month prior to the submission of the project report, presentation sessions are arranged so that each student can talk about their project and receive feedback from peers and lecturers.
6. The student completes the project report, which is graded by the advisor.

7. The module coordinator reads the project reports and serves as a double marker.

Following the project

8. The module coordinator considers comments from the project advisors and the external examiner (who will have reviewed several project reports), and identifies means for improving future project work.

9. The ideas identified in step 8 are communicated to staff and students in the following year for their consideration.

Supporting materials	□ No particular materials are required.

Outcomes worth noting	□ Staff can gain a better understanding of students' work and abilities through students' presentations. □ Students can receive feedback on multiple occasions and from various sources. □ External examiners' comments are used to improve the process.

Student response	□ "I have benefited greatly from my own independent learning and discussions with my advisor." □ "Through the process of systematic learning and searching for materials, I have acquired a deep understanding of my topic." □ "The workload involved in completing this project far exceeds the credit points allocated; the project should carry more credit points."

How this practice supports learning	• Three opportunities for feedback from a variety of sources are provided: (i) from the advisor, (ii) from the expert guests, and (iii) from peers and lecturers. • This feedback is provided at critical stages in the project when the student is in a good position to act on it — at the beginning when the project is still being formulated, and towards the end, when students are highly motivated to complete the project and write it up. • The presentation session is likely to (i) motivate students to clarify their ideas, (ii) help them to review their sense of standards that are both required and possible as they compare their work with that of their peers, and (iii) provide useful ideas in the form of feedback from peers and teachers.

Further suggestions	This is a time-intensive, highly individualized practice. In other situations, the following could be considered: • Clear and detailed guidelines provided at the beginning of the process may reduce the need for consultation.

Learning Autonomously

- Parts of the process could be conducted online, including receiving and responding to initial proposals and ongoing progress reports.
- Some ongoing support could be provided by students working in small groups, face-to-face or online, for the purpose of sharing ideas and giving each other feedback.
- Students working in similar areas could consult specialist experts in groups.

Contributor

Louisa LAM

Department of Mathematics

The Hong Kong Institute of Education

Email: llam@ied.edu.hk

30. Automated feedback on case studies

Shekhar KUMTA, The Chinese University of Hong Kong

Summary
Key features of this online assessment format include the use of case studies and automated feedback in the form of reflective questions and suggestions. Each case study develops through a sequence of scenarios presented in words, pictures, numbers or diagrams. Students work independently through the situations in sequence and answer a multiple choice question for each situation. Only the correct answer leads to the next stage in the sequence. Learning takes place when automated feedback guides students to the correct answer.

Situations where this practice could be used
- This practice could be used in any discipline where students could learn autonomously from a sequence of problem-solving situations.
- This practice is especially suitable for experienced teachers who are familiar with the types of problems students are likely to experience.

Background	One critical element in the education of health care professionals is the development of clinical decision making skills, which are honed on working with a large number of real-life cases. This practice provides real-life cases online. Students have more opportunities to develop their clinical decision making skills than they would have normally through clinical attachments alone.
Rationale	This practice aims to □ develop clinical decision-making skills; □ develop independent, lifelong learning skills such as reflection; and □ provide immediate feedback in a non-threatening online environment at a time and place suited to the learner.
Procedure	1. Final-year medical students are introduced to a series of web-based case studies during a four-week module. 2. Each case study develops through a sequence of scenarios presented in words, pictures, numbers and diagrams. 3. Students navigate through the situations and answer a multiple choice question for each situation. By the end of a case study, students would have answered three to five key questions at focal points within the case. 4. Students are given appropriate automatic feedback whenever an incorrect response is made. This helps them to understand the basis of their error and enables them to successfully complete a case.

Learning Autonomously

5. Teachers are able to identify students with learning difficulties and key areas where such difficulties exist. A timely remedial intervention is thus possible.

Supporting materials	□	This practice requires a web site with a series of carefully designed case studies. In the present case, a web site at the Chinese University of Hong Kong has been designed for this purpose.
Outcomes worth noting	□	Students with major learning difficulties can be identified and remedial measures instituted.
	□	Students are prompted to visit wards more often and stimulated to engage in more clinical interaction.
	□	Online feedback is especially welcomed by students who are not yet comfortable with answering questions during face-to-face ward visits.
Student response	□	Students have reported (through class surveys) that the online case studies are a useful learning resource and want more of these in the various disciplines within their medical studies.
	□	Students have also reported that some problems could only be solved in face-to-face tutorials.

How this practice supports learning	• Students usually find case studies relevant, challenging, and satisfying.
	• Case studies such as these typically require a good understanding of concepts and procedures, thereby encouraging students to develop this understanding through independent study.
	• The case studies are spread across four weeks, requiring students to spend a reasonable amount of time on this highly relevant form of study.
	• Generating automated feedback for addressing errors or problems should be cost-effective in the long run.

Further suggestions	• Feedback can direct students to further information such as textbooks or more detailed web-based information.
	• Students could contribute to the development of new cases based on their clinical experiences. This will help their own development as well as reducing the demands on the staff in developing new cases.

Contributor

Shekhar KUMTA

The Chinese University of Hong Kong

Email: kumta@cuhk.edu.hk

Learning Autonomously

▌ **Evaluating Oneself** ▌

31. Ungraded tasks leading to summative assignments

LIU Pui Lee, The Hong Kong Institute of Education

Summary
Participants in an in-service education programme find various kinds of learning resources such as articles, lesson plans, and task samples from the library and the language centre, for discussion in class. They accumulate these resources and write reflections on them as part of their own portfolios. The portfolio acts as a reference that documents what they have learned and constitutes an important resource to use in their summative assignments.

Situations where this practice could be used
This practice could be used in any context where students need to locate relevant materials for later assignments and where the sharing of those materials with fellow students is seen to promote learning.

Background	This practice has been used in in-service education programmes for teachers.
Rationale	Students are often required to complete summative assignments at the end of a module. How to build up what they have learned during the module and apply this to the assignment is an important issue. In this practice, participant teachers develop a portfolio to document their learning process and to build up what they have learned. These portfolios serve the purposes of a collection of resources for helping teachers so that they can more effectively complete their summative assignment.
Procedure	1. In-service teachers are introduced to various kinds of teaching resources, such as lesson plans, learning tasks and web sites.
	2. They are asked to select and bring to each class meeting one or two such teaching resources to introduce to their classmates.
	3. Each class meeting is divided into two sessions. In the first session, students are engaged in reflective workshops related to teaching issues. In the second session, they discuss the teaching resources they have identified. They briefly share with their classmates why they have chosen the teaching resources and how they intend to use them with their own school students.
	4. They then write a reflection to evaluate what they have learned, based on the workshop, discussion and feedback from their peers and lecturer (Appendix 1).

Evaluating Oneself
▌

5. They select and organize the teaching resources and reflection into a portfolio to demonstrate what they have learned.

6. None of the tasks outlined above is graded. However, the portfolio is used as a reference/resource by students for a summative assignment at the end of the module.

7. The summative assignment of the module requires teachers to design lesson plans related to current trends in educational reform. They are able to utilize the teaching resources that they have collected for the portfolio and the reflections that have been promoted. There is thus integration between the ungraded portfolio and the lesson plans required for the summative assignment (Appendix 2).

Supporting materials	☐	Participants need ready access to a range of library, Internet and other resources.
Outcomes worth noting	☐	Participants seem to find the discussion and sharing sessions and the associated tasks worthwhile.
	☐	The process of locating resources and developing the portfolio can foster participants' reflection.
	☐	Most importantly, these ungraded tasks build up to a 'portfolio' which participants draw on for their end-of-module summative assignment. Some teachers also use this portfolio to share with their school colleagues and principals what they have done and learnt in the module, thus bridging the gulf between a course and on-site professional practice.
Student response	☐	"When I select the artefacts to put into my portfolio, I have to look back at what I have learned, and select those artefacts that represent my learning. When comparing the artefacts, it can stimulate my reflection."
	☐	"I discuss my task samples (the learning evidence) with my peers and the lecturer. They give me feedback and such feedback can stimulate me to reflect on how I can improve, which helps me to do the assignment."
	☐	"Although I benefit from reading more tasks samples, I don't have enough time to do so. It is quite time-consuming to find the articles and task samples to put into the portfolio."
	☐	"I don't really understand how to develop the portfolio; I need more guidelines."

How this practice supports learning	• This practice involves students in working through the semester, rather than concentrating their effort around the time of the final assignment. • The social context of the class, and the requirement to present findings, is likely to ensure that the work is done for the class. • This preparatory work seems highly appropriate for the subject area, and students are likely to appreciate that it will contribute to their final assignment. • The process generates a climate of discussion, sharing, feedback and reflection on ongoing work.

Further suggestions	• The developing portfolios could be the basis of structured peer feedback at particular stages of the module. • A process for publicly sharing portfolios with class members at the completion of the module could be particularly useful for participants in such in-service programmes. They could use this process, once their work has been marked, to enhance their own set of resources for use in their workplace. • Placing portfolios on a course web site could facilitate teacher and peer access to them. • Examples of portfolios could be made available to future cohorts of students (with the originators' permission) to provide further guidance regarding the expected nature and extent of portfolios.

Contributor

LIU Pui Lee
Department of Chinese
The Hong Kong Institute of Education
Email: plliu@ied.edu.hk

Evaluating Oneself

APPENDIX 1

Reflective worksheet

1. How have you benefited from the workshop?

2. How have you benefited from the discussion of the articles and the task samples?

3. Have you encountered any problem that you don't understand? How can you solve the problem?

4. What are the important points that you want to write down that can help you to do the assignment?

5. What is your feeling/reflection about this meeting?

APPENDIX 2

The assignment task (the summative assignment)

Participants are asked to develop the unit of lesson plans related to the current education reforms that enhance students' reading, writing, speaking and listening skills in Chinese language.

How the module is conducted

Session	Theme	Organization of the sessions
1	Introduction	Introduce the module, the new trend of teaching Chinese in primary schools and how to develop the portfolios. Participants are expected to find various kinds of teaching resources in the language centre before each session.
2–3	Reading task	Sessions 2 to 9 of the module are conducted as follows:
4–5	Speaking task	1. Mini-lectures about the theory of reading/speaking/writing/listening aspects in teaching Chinese language (about 15 minutes). 2. Workshops for participants to develop language tasks in groups.
6–7	Writing task	3. Discussion of the readings, articles and tasks collected during self-study, and criteria for evaluating tasks.
8–9	Listening task	For all sessions, time is provided for participants to write their reflections in the worksheet and develop the portfolios.
10	Conclusion	Participants look back on their portfolios and conclude what they learn such as the criteria of evaluating different learning tasks. They can make use of the collection of learning evidence in the portfolios as references, helping them to do the summative assignments a month after the module finishes.

Evaluating Oneself

32. Helping students diagnose and track error patterns in written work

Icy LEE, The University of Hong Kong

Summary
This assessment technique facilitates error feedback by helping students become more aware of their prevalent error patterns in writing. Comprehensive error feedback is provided on students' first assignment for diagnostic purposes, so that students are made aware of the most serious error types in their work. In subsequent assignments, students engage in self and peer evaluation, learning to take greater responsibility for learning by analysing and correcting their recurrent errors.

Situations where this practice could be used
- This practice could be applied to many situations where students are likely to commit a range of predictable errors in a written assignment.
- This practice has specific application in language learning situations, where commonly made grammatical and other errors are readily identified and described.

Background	This practice has been used in English language courses, both English as a first language and English as second language.
Rationale	Teachers can often predict the kinds of mistakes their students are likely to make in their written work and they can spend a large amount of time providing feedback on such errors. Yet these errors often resurface again and again. This technique seeks to develop students' independence in identifying, analysing and correcting their own errors in writing.
Procedure	1. The tutor prepares a list of common error categories (see Appendix 1). Students' self and peer evaluation of errors is based on the tutor's list of common errors.
	2. Students submit their first assignment for diagnostic purposes.
	3. The tutor numbers all the errors in each student assignment (#1, #2, etc.) and responds to the written errors in detail, based on the list of common error categories. The tutor enters the results in an error analysis sheet (see Appendix 2), correcting the errors for students or asking students to correct their own errors.
	4. The tutor then summarizes the results of this error analysis in a summary form and passes it to the students (see Appendix 3). From the summary of error types, error ratio and error gravity ranking, students identify the most serious error types for themselves.
	5. The summaries of individual results can help the tutor identify the

Evaluating Oneself

needs of the whole class. The tutor can then design grammar instruction to cater to the students' needs.

6. In each of the subsequent assignments, students engage in self-evaluation before submitting their work, analysing error types and correcting errors in their own writing.

7. Students also exchange assignments with their peers, helping each other identify, analyse and correct errors.

8. Finally, students enter the results of their analysis (based on self and/or peer evaluation) for each assignment in an error analysis sheet and review how much progress they have made and what areas they need to work on further.

Supporting materials	☐ See Appendices.
Outcomes worth noting	☐ Students are less reliant on the tutor for correcting their errors. ☐ Students develop greater independence in self-editing.
Student response	☐ Students think that this technique can help raise their awareness of the errors that they may make in writing and in the long run reduce errors made. ☐ Some students are worried that they do not have adequate knowledge of grammar to identify, categorize and correct errors for themselves. ☐ Doing self-evaluation and/or peer evaluation on a regular basis could be perceived as tedious, and some students may not have the incentive to do so. ☐ This technique suits self-motivated learners better.

How this practice supports learning	• The initial assignment is purely diagnostic. From this, tutors are able to identify errors that are commonly made in their classes and can use this information to plan their subsequent teaching. It is important to know student misunderstandings and to address these directly. • The error analysis form gives students a clear and objective basis for evaluating the grammatical accuracy of their own and their fellow students' work. By using this technique regularly, students develop a sense of the standard required and are able to judge their work against this. • Students learn from each others' errors, and the frequency that these errors occur, and gain an appreciation of the relative importance of different kinds of errors in their writing. • This self and peer editing process helps students to internalize criteria and required standards and provides rapid and timely feedback on written errors.

Evaluating Oneself

Further suggestions	• Tutors could use only some of the procedures in this practice. For example, they could simply distribute a list of common errors for students to use before they submit an assignment. This list could be the basis of a self-editing, or could be used for peer editing prior to submission.
	• Students could be involved in formulating an initial list of errors. For example, in a whole-class situation, students could be given three examples of writing: a good one, a poor one and an intermediate one. They could then be asked to identify the errors which made the worst one poor, and then compare the errors they had identified in it with those other students had discovered. This could be the basis for an error list of their own.

Contributor

Icy LEE

The University of Hong Kong

Email: icylee@hkucc.hku.hk

APPENDIX 1

List of Common Error Categories

1. Verb tense	8. Noun endings
2. Verb form	9. Comma splices
3. Articles/determiners	10. Sentence fragments
4. Pronouns	11. Sentence pattern
5. Subject-verb agreement	12. Spelling
6. Word form	13. Punctuation
7. Word choice	14. Others

Evaluating Oneself

APPENDIX 2

Teacher Analysis of Error Types for the First Written Assignment

Error Number	Type of Error	Correction
#1	Subject–verb agreement	The news <u>is</u> shocking.
#2	Spelling	Environment
#3		
#4		
#5		
#6		
#7		
#8		
#9		
#10		

APPENDIX 3

Summary of Error Patterns for the First Written Assignment (For Teacher's Use)

Student name:

Error type	Number of errors made	Error ratio★	Error gravity ranking★★
Verb tense	4	0.2	2
Verb form	3	0.15	3
Articles/determiners	8	0.4	1
Pronouns	–	–	–
Subject–verb agreement	2	0.1	4
Word form	3	0.15	3
Word choice	–	–	–
Noun endings	–	–	–
Comma splices	–	–	–
Sentence fragments	–	–	–
Sentence pattern	–	–	–
Spelling	–	–	–
Punctuation	–	–	–
Others	–	–	–
Total number of errors	20		

★   Error ratio = Divide the number of errors in each category by the total errors (i.e. the larger the ratio, the more serious the error)

★★ Mark '1' for the most serious error type, then '2', '3', and so on. Mark 'NA' if there is no error in a particular

33. Engagement with assessment criteria for self-assessment

David CARLESS, The University of Hong Kong

Summary
Students analyse the assessment criteria for their assignment by carrying out a short in-class activity in which they summarize the key points in the criteria. Building on this activity, students are required to submit (as part of their assignment), their own self-assessment checklist. This process both makes the criteria more meaningful to students and encourages them to self-evaluate their own performance in relation to their interpretation of the criteria.

Situations where this practice could be used
This generic technique is especially suitable for the liberal arts and humanities, where qualitative judgement is often based on criteria that are fuzzy rather than sharp and where students tend to work privately and do not usually have the opportunity to see or read the work of peers.

Background	☐ This technique has been used in teacher education courses on a number of different modules and topics.
	☐ The version described here was used with a group of Bachelor of Education students studying a module on the topic of Assessment in English language teaching. Their assignment was to design assessment tasks for primary school learners and write a rationale (Appendix 1).
Rationale	☐ Descriptive statements of criteria are often not very helpful to students because they do not have the tacit knowledge that teachers have to interpret these statements. This technique helps students to become clearer about the assessment criteria and the characteristics of good and less successful assignments.
	☐ The technique makes the assessment and marking process more transparent to students.
	☐ The technique helps students to self-evaluate their own work as a lifelong learning strategy and as a specific means of enhancing the quality of their assignment.
Procedure	1. Students are provided with the module assignment details and the assessment criteria in the first session of the module.
	2. In the third session (once students have got a flavour of the content of the module), the lecturer provides an initial explanation of the requirements of the module assignment.
	3. Students are then provided with the assessment criteria (Appendix 2) for a certain grade e.g. B grade (seen as representing a reasonable target for many students). They study the statements and individually identify

Evaluating Oneself

the key points and summarize in their own words the five to six characteristics which are needed for a B-grade assignment (Appendix 3).

4. A brief discussion is carried out to try to ensure that students are aware of the characteristics of good/less good assignments.

5. The tutor explains to students that they can use the criteria to monitor their own performance and identify their strengths and weaknesses. By doing this effectively, they have the potential to increase their own grade.

6. As part of their assignment, students are required to include a self-assessment of their own work (related to the criteria). The requirement of including a self-assessment is reflected in the rubric.

Supporting materials	See Appendices.
Outcomes worth noting	☐ Students understand better how grades are awarded and so the marking process becomes more transparent. ☐ Students become more aware of the criteria and the characteristics of good work. ☐ Some students become more sensitized to the strengths and weaknesses of their own work, whilst others still find it challenging to self-evaluate perceptively.
Student response	☐ "When designing the self-evaluation sheet, I have to refer back to the criteria and then check with my assignment. I think this acts as a double-checking. Before, I seldom check my assignments deeply." ☐ "I think I am responsible for my own learning because of more proofreading. I can try to make changes in my assignment based on my own evaluation before I hand in the assignment." ☐ "I find it hard to understand criteria as they are full of jargon terms. Sometimes I try to guess what the lecturer is looking for from what he says in class."

How this practice supports learning	• This practice engages students in communication about what constitutes high-quality work. • Students are helped towards understanding the criteria which tutors will apply to their work. • When students have worked at interpreting the meaning of the criteria, they develop a greater sense of ownership of the criteria, allowing them to work harder towards demonstrating their achievement of the criteria in their work. • This practice supports students in self-evaluation and requires them to reflect on their work.

Evaluating Oneself

- This practice enables students to identify their own areas for improvement.

Further suggestions	• The tutor could distribute real examples of A-grade, B-grade and E-grade work. Students study these and different groups of students are given different characteristics to identify. They then present their 'findings' to the whole class. This process links criteria to standards in a concrete way. Students could also apply the criteria against samples of work. • Students could be involved in generating the criteria, possibly using good and poor examples of work as above as a starting point. • The self-assessment process could be supplemented by peer assessment. • Students could be given examples of criteria as used by tutors, and asked to jot down their responses to 'what this really means is ... .' for each criterion, then compare their responses and work towards an agreed meaning for each criterion in turn.

Contributor

David CARLESS

The University of Hong Kong

Email: dcarless@hkucc.hku.hk

Evaluating Oneself

APPENDIX 1

Assignment task

Develop a 'formative' or 'alternative assessment' task for use with a specified group of primary school students. State the rationale for the task and how it is based on learning theories and/or the current educational reform, where appropriate.

How does the assessment support learning? What are the specific difficulties that students are likely to face in doing the assessment task and how might a teacher support their learning, before or after they do the assessments?

Include a self-assessment of your work as an Appendix.

APPENDIX 2

B grade criteria reproduced

The assessment tasks are quite well-designed and show an understanding of good assessment practices. The rationale is reasonably clear and quite well-written and there is evidence of a knowledge of relevant literature, well-referenced. The relationship between assessment and pupil learning is indicated quite well. The assignment contains a quite well-designed self-assessment sheet.

There is a high degree of accuracy in the assessment tasks. For prose parts, a wide range of simple and complex structures are used reasonably successfully and grammatical structures are usually accurate with communication not impeded.

APPENDIX 3

Understanding assessment criteria

Task 1   Study the criteria for B grade. Identify in note form in your own words, five to six characteristics which are needed for a B assignment.

Evaluating Oneself

1.
2.
3.
4.
5.
6.

Follow-up

Your self-assessment for your assignment needs to be related to achieving the criteria.

34. Helping students to self-assess their learning needs

LUNG Ching Leung and Magdalena Mo Ching MOK, The Hong Kong Institute of Education

Summary
'Know-want-learn' (KWL) is a method that supports students' self-assessment. It has three components: self-assessment and reflection on what the student already *knows* about the topic before learning (K); based on the self-assessment, reflection upon what the student *wants* to learn (W); and self-assessment and reflection upon what has been learned after the teaching session (L).

Situations where this practice could be used
This technique can be used in the liberal arts and humanities, where what is already known and what is new is not so easily separated. It is also likely to be useful in mathematics, science and engineering disciplines, and medical education, where it is equally important to allow students to see that they are continuously building upon what they already know. It is particularly suited to teaching situations that are relatively structured (such as lectures) with clearly defined topics and objectives.

Background	This technique has been applied in teacher education programmes.
Rationale	The KWL has foundations in learning psychology (Ogle, 1986; Carr and Ogle, 1987):

□ The Know (K) component is designed to tap students' prior knowledge, which is one of the most important factors in subsequent learning. Self-assessment of prior knowledge helps the learner to consolidate what has been learned and provides a strong schema for new learning.

□ The Want (W) component is designed to help students set their learning goals, thereby establishing the need and motivation for learning.

□ The Learn (L) component helps students' self-assessment of what has been learned in order to consolidate the newly learnt knowledge through explicit articulation.

Procedure	1. Students are invited to reflect on the question 'What do you already know about the concept?' at the beginning of the lecture. This helps students to gauge their prior knowledge, and alerts lecturers to the level and range of students' prior learning.
	2. At the beginning and during the lecture, students are invited to reflect on the question, 'What do you want to know about the concept?' This aims to heighten learning motivation, allowing students a greater sense of ownership of what they wish to achieve through the lecture.

Evaluating Oneself

3. At the end of the lecture students are invited to reflect on the question, 'What have you learned about the concept?' This helps students to assess and reflect on their own learning, and allows the lecturer to gain data about the learning which was actually achieved by means of the lecture.

4. The lecturer analyses students' responses to align his or her teaching with the learning that is taking place, students' 'wants', and other gaps in learning.

5. The lecturer can summarize responses from all students in the group and provide feedback to the group, or use some of the responses as stimuli for class discussion and collective reflection. This step provides further opportunities to support students' metacognition.

Supporting materials	Various supporting worksheets can be used. The sample (Appendix) was used in an Education Project module in which pre-service teacher education students were preparing a small-scale piece of educational research. Students complete questions 1 and 2 at the outset of the lecture, and question 3 at the conclusion of the session and then hand it in to the lecturer.
Outcomes worth noting	☐ Student surveys suggest that students' metacognition is more developed after using the KWL method and that they gain in interest and understanding of the subject matter. Students have also indicated that the method is helpful to their learning and self-assessment. ☐ Lecturers have found the KWL method helpful in building metacognition about their teaching and providing valuable information about student learning. ☐ Although the KWL method is easy to administer, lecturers find the analysis time-consuming and demanding, particularly if they choose to implement changes in response to students' feedback.
Student response	☐ "I know what prior knowledge I possess and I could organize my concepts in my mind ... ." ☐ "... I am clear about my expectation on learning, and thus I could define a learning goal." ☐ "It helps me develop a habit to ask myself what I have learned." ☐ "It takes me much time to fill in the worksheet and to think, affecting the progress of the lesson."
How this practice supports learning	• Students' confidence can be increased through reflecting on what they already know about a topic, and comparing what they know to what other students know. In particular, their confidence can be further developed by finding out that other students share similar 'want to know' aspects relating to the subject of the lecture.

Evaluating Oneself

- This technique encourages students to develop a habit of reflecting on what it is of significance that they still need to learn. Used in conjunction with assessed tasks that have clearly identified criteria and standards, the technique can help students to focus their study efforts on material that will be most useful for them in meeting assessment requirements.
- Reflecting on exactly what they have learned from a lecture helps students to deepen their learning of the concepts involved, and encourages them to become more conscious of how they are continuing to learn in future lectures.

Further suggestions	<ul><li>Students can be asked to relate their learning to explicit criteria and standards that are being applied in a course. For example, they could be asked to complete a self-assessment pro forma near the start of a lecture and to explore (for example) the extent to which they could already demonstrate their achievement of some of the intended learning outcomes associated with the lecture.</li><li>The technique could be used selectively with topics where it is seen to be particularly relevant, for example, where students are known to have done significant previous study.</li><li>Students could be issued with a further self-assessment pro forma after particular lectures, to allow them to reflect on the extent to which they now felt able to demonstrate their achievement of the intended learning outcomes of these lectures.</li><li>The technique could be simplified. In the case described here, the process was carried out comprehensively as part of research into teaching and learning, reported in Mok et al. (2006).</li></ul>

References

Carr, E., and Ogle, D. (1987) K-W-L plus: A strategy for comprehension and summarization. *Journal of Reading*, 30, 626–31.

Mok, M., Lung, C. L., Cheng, P. W., Cheung, H. P., and Ng, M. L. (2006) Self-assessment in higher education: Experience in using a metacognitive approach in five case studies. *Assessment and Evaluation in Higher Education*, 31(4), 415–33.

Ogle, D. (1986) K-W-L: A teaching model that develops active reading in expository text. *The Reading Teacher*, 39, 564–76.

Contributors

LUNG Ching Leung and Magdalena Mo Ching MOK
The Hong Kong Institute of Education
Email: cllung@ied.edu.hk; mmcmok@ied.edu.hk

Evaluating Oneself

Evaluating Oneself

APPENDIX

School of Foundations in Education
Two-Year Full-Time Bachelor of Education (Honours)(Primary) Programme
Education Project (Phase 1)

Name: _____ Student No.: _____ Date: _____ Lecture: _____ Literature Review: _____

As a self-regulated learner, please reflect upon the following 3 questions:

What do I already know about this topic?
What do I want to know in this topic?
What have I learned about this topic?

1. What do I already know about literature review?	2. What do I want to know about literature review?	3. What have I learnt about literature review?

▌ Processing and Acting on Feedback ▌

---

35. Ensuring that students process and act on feedback

Learning to Learn Course Team, City University of Hong Kong

Summary
This assessment technique invites students to indicate the extent to which they agree with teachers' feedback on their coursework and how they plan to improve their work. Students need to discuss their responses to feedback with their peers before submitting a brief written response to the teacher.

Situations where this practice could be used
This practice could be applied in any course where students are given feedback that can be used to improve the quality of their subsequent work within the course.

Background   The *Learning to Learn* Course at City University of Hong Kong has adopted a problem-based learning environment to develop students' deep approaches to learning. To support a deep approach to learning, a combination of self, peer and teacher assessment is used. As a key part of the assessment process, students are required to discuss and respond to teacher feedback on assignments.

Rationale   □   Teacher feedback may not necessarily help students to learn better or produce better work — students often do not treat teacher feedback seriously and no actions for improvement are taken. Some students do not understand the feedback they receive, or they may not agree with it. However, they seldom discuss this with their teacher.

□   This simple technique invites students to respond to their teacher's feedback. This practice ensures that the feedback is received by the student, that it is attended to, and that it is acted on. The practice also promotes interaction between student and teacher.

Procedure   1.   Students submit their assignments.
2.   Teachers mark the assignments, provide written feedback, and return them to the students.
3.   Students analyse the teacher's feedback and write a response to indicate
     (a) the extent to which they agree with the feedback; and
     (b) what they will do to develop themselves as better learners.
4.   Students discuss their responses with peers before submitting a written version to their teacher.
5.   Teachers respond to the student responses if necessary.

Supporting materials	Suggested questions to guide student responses:
	☐ Do you agree with the teacher's feedback? To what extent?
	☐ Which parts you tend to agree with? Why?
	☐ Which parts you tend to disagree with? Why?
	☐ How can you do better next time?
	☐ What are your plans for improvement?
Outcomes worth noting	☐ Students have become more attentive to teacher feedback rather than focusing solely on grades.
	☐ Students' metacognitive ability to monitor their own learning has been developed.
	☐ Students have become more engaged in learning and high-quality coursework has been produced as a result.
	☐ Teachers note that this scheme has increased their communication with students, leading to a better understanding of their students.
	☐ Teachers are able to trace their students' development and can therefore give more individualized feedback.
Student response	☐ "I have become more attentive to teacher feedback."
	☐ "This system provides me with an opportunity to discuss my assignments with peers and teachers."
	☐ "… creates a good learning atmosphere"
	☐ "I can learn how to be a critical friend to help peers learn better."
	☐ "Motivating but also time demanding."

How this practice supports learning	• This practice goes to the heart of feedback and how it can be used to support students' learning. The social context of discussing feedback with peers provides students with a good opportunity to discuss their work with their colleagues. Students may often find it easier to discuss this initially with their peers than with their teacher.
	• The need to provide a written response to the teacher ensures that students have reviewed their feedback and gives the teacher an opportunity for further dialogue with the student if this is required.
	• By making discussion of tutor feedback a required task, it becomes impossible for the student to ignore it.

Further suggestions	• The limited amount of time teachers typically have to meet with individual students makes peer discussion a useful alternative means for students to think further about their own work, and the opportunity to discuss their fellow student's work may develop a new perspective on their own work.

Processing and Acting on Feedback

- The procedure could be extended to require students to apply the feedback in their next piece of work.
- Students could be asked to complete an assignment submission sheet with their assignments that mirrors the marking sheet the tutor uses, and to complete it giving estimations of how well they have achieved against each criterion. The tutor can review this after completing his/her own assessment, and look for gaps in understanding between the student's estimation and the tutor's.

Contributors

Learning to Learn Course Team
Contact person: Anna Siu-fong KWAN
City University of Hong Kong
Email: anna.kwan@cityu.edu.hk

36. Tutorial review of draft assignments: Dialogue and reflection

Rita BERRY, The Hong Kong Institute of Education

Summary
Before a tutorial, students send the tutor their first draft of an assignment from which the tutor identifies points that need discussion. During the tutorial, non-directive feedback is provided, focusing on helping students to be aware of the issues they need to address if they want to improve their work. At the end of the session, a 'quiet time' for reflection is available for students to consider the issues discussed and to write down the points they regard as being key to improving their work. Students act upon the decisions they make and revise their work based on their understanding of the points made during the interactive session.

Situations where this practice could be used
This technique can be applied in any situation where students are able to seek feedback on draft assignments.

Background	This practice has been used with students in the third year of a four-year bachelor of education programme. It focuses on an essay in which students report on and critically analyse curriculum implementation in a school.
Rationale	☐ Students who are more able to take responsibility for their own learning are usually more successful learners.
	☐ The opportunities for thinking embedded in an interactive tutorial session enable students to take initiative in raising questions for discussion.
	☐ The end-of-session quiet time allows students to recall the points discussed and make decisions on what they deem useful for their own learning.
Procedure	*Before the tutorial*
	1. The students submit the first draft of their work.
	2. Before the interactive discussion session, the tutor quickly reads the work and highlights the specific areas which need to be improved.
	During the tutorial
	3. Students attend an individual or a group tutorial.
	• During an individual tutorial, the tutor first invites the student to make an educated guess why the areas on his or her own scripts are highlighted. The tutor then gives feedback to the student on his/her self-assessment. The student can ask for further feedback from the tutor as a basis for further discussion.
	• For a group tutorial, the tutor similarly invites the students to self-

Processing and Acting on Feedback

assess their work based on the highlighted aspects. The self-assessment will then lead into a peer assessment with the tutor as the facilitator. When encountering some issues which students cannot resolve themselves, they can ask the tutor for feedback.

4. The students take notes of the feedback from their peers and the tutor puts the notes in the first box of the feedback form.

5. The students sit in a quiet corner and recall the issues discussed. They write down the specific areas they think would help improve their work in the second box of the feedback form.

6. The tutor keeps a copy of the completed feedback form.

After the tutorial

7. The students revise the first draft of their work with the points noted down in the feedback form.

8. Students submit the final draft of their work. The tutor grades the work in the normal way.

9. (Optional) Students compare the two drafts and reflect on the improvements they have made.

Supporting materials	□ Feedback Form (see Appendix).
Outcomes worth noting	□ Students become more aware of the benefit they can gain by taking greater responsibility for their own learning.
	□ Immediate feedback is made available in the tutorial session. Students can seek answers or directions from the tutor.
	□ What is expected of students can be made clear to them through the interactive tutorial session.
	□ Feedback requested by the students is more effective than feedback simply given directly by the tutor.
	□ The quiet time is very useful as it allows students to conceptualize the issues discussed and decide on the next step to take.
	□ As individual consultation is time-consuming, group consultation can be used as an alternative in larger classes.
Student response	□ "My tutor's feedback enabled me to identify the problems of my essay. During the feedback session, I was encouraged to make suggestions about how the problems could be solved."
	□ "I could redraft my essay right away."
	□ "I think this kind of two-way communication is good for improving my work. Interaction always triggers critical thinking."
	□ "I think group feedback is beneficial. But it is difficult to do well."
	□ "Useful, but in such a rush, I don't have time to think through my mistakes."

Processing and Acting on Feedback

How this practice supports learning	• Providing feedback on draft work is an important opportunity for dialogue with students and for providing 'feedforward', that is, suggestions that students can use in a subsequent draft. This can be extremely time-consuming when done on an individual basis, but much less so if done in a tutorial.
	• The simple technique of having students quietly review their assignment and the tutorial feedback within the tutorial session ensures that they have applied the general feedback to their own work.
	• By leaving a copy of the feedback form with the tutor, students are encouraged to incorporate feedback in their final version, knowing that their tutor may check whether they have done so.
	• This technique also provides an opportunity for students to consider the standards expected in the assignment and to assess their work against those standards. Discussion also allows them to see aspects of how their peers are dealing with the assignment and therefore to consider alternative approaches in their own work.

Further suggestions	• Students could be offered group tutorials only. This would ensure that they would benefit from each other's feedback as well as from the tutor's. It would also require less of the tutor's time.
	• Students in the group tutorial could initiate the process by highlighting matters for discussion rather than the tutor taking the lead in this. The tutor can then add his or her ideas. This also reduces the pressure on the tutor, while increasing the students' responsibility.
	• Tutors could respond electronically to early-draft submissions submitted by email, using the 'Notes' or 'Comment' function in Word.

Contributor
Rita BERRY
Department of Curriculum and Instruction
The Hong Kong Institute of Education
Email: rsyberry@ied.edu.hk

Processing and Acting on Feedback

APPENDIX

Feedback form

Student name: _____   Date and Time: _____

Programme: _____   Module: _____

1.   Interactive session

Please put your notes here.

2.   Quiet time

Please put down the specific areas you think would help improve your work.

37. Staged assessment and feedback

Frankie Yuen Yee YU, The Hong Kong Institute of Education

Summary

This assessment technique turns a substantial assignment into six manageable small assignments. It focuses on learning, assessing and re-learning small chunks of knowledge as students complete the large assignment in stages. Timely feedback with the tutor at each stage is especially designed for students who need it most. Students can use verbal and written comments to revise and resubmit their work.

Situations where this practice could be used

This practice could be used in any discipline where classes are relatively small and continuous assessment does not create an unrealistic marking and supervision load.

Background

The assessment for the module Primary Chinese Teaching Methodology previously required students to design a lesson plan at the end of the module. However, the quality of work of students was typically not good and they faced many difficulties when working on the assignment. This assessment technique is a response to this particular problem. It replaces the end-of-module assignment with small assignments spread over the duration of the module.

Rationale

This practice seeks to

☐ sequence learning and assessment to provide knowledge building, i.e., 'scaffolding';

☐ give timely feedback to provide opportunities for 're-learning' or consolidation, so that students are better motivated to submit assignments of high quality; and

☐ instil in students a sense of pride in or appreciation of their own work.

Procedure

1. The assignment is divided into six parts, according to the structure of a lesson plan: objectives, motivation, comprehension, vocabulary, in-depth studies and exercises.

2. Students complete one part and their work is graded before they attempt the next part.

3. Good work is showcased and discussed in class by the tutor.

4. Students study specific comments, reflect on their work and make suggestions for improvement.

5. Students who are awarded Grade D or below are required to discuss their suggestions for improvement with the tutor. Consultation with the tutor is optional for students who get Grade C or above.

Processing and Acting on Feedback

6. At each stage, students can revise and re-submit their work.
7. The end product is a lesson plan.

Supporting materials	None.
Outcomes worth noting	□ Staged assessment helps learning since difficulties are dealt with at each stage and feedback helps 're-learning' and consolidation. □ Students are more motivated and confident. □ Some students make improvements and some focus simply on getting higher grades. □ This practice can be demanding for the tutor since many students may need face-to-face feedback.
Student response	□ Students who improve and re-submit their work develop a better understanding of the design of a lesson plan. □ Students agree that consultation with the tutor helps in solving their problems. □ Students are positive about the tutor's comments and agree that feedback stimulates their thinking and reflection. □ More time is spent on assignments but students generally consider this worthwhile.
How this practice supports learning	• The staged assessment tasks avoid heavy end-of-module workloads and engage students in productive learning activity that spreads time and effort evenly across the module. • Students are able to act upon the feedback in order to improve their ongoing work, and enhance their learning. • More intense interactions with staff foster a community of learning that encourages independence and responsibility. • Students are more likely to see assessment as a partnership activity, rather than one in which they are merely passive recipients of judgements.
Further suggestions	• The heavy demand on tutor time could be alleviated if peer feedback, preferably before the assignment is graded, can be gradually introduced. • This approach is particularly suitable for the early stages of a programme where intensive support can minimize failure and drop-out.

Processing and Acting on Feedback

Contributor

Frankie Yuen Yee YU
The Hong Kong Institute of Education
Email: fryu@ied.edu.hk

38. Cycles of feedback in an assessment task

Ina SIU, The Hong Kong Institute of Education

Summary

This assessment strategy attempts to break the traditional divisions between assessment, teaching and learning by integrating the assessment task into the teaching sessions and building in regular tutor and peer feedback in the learning process for helping students to improve their performance in the assessment.

Situations where this practice could be used

This practice could be used in most situations involving oral presentations to a class.

Background	This practice is used in a first-year English module in a pre-service Bachelor of Education programme.
Rationale	Assessment is always an important element in the teaching and learning process. However, it often happens at the very end of the cycle. When it does, useful feedback based on assessment results and weaknesses that are revealed in the final assessment will have little impact on learning. Eventually, students will view assessment as purely evaluation of their own performance and not feedback on their learning. This practice integrates assessment into the teaching process to help students assimilate what they are learning in the theoretical input of the module and through tutor and peer feedback, to integrate learning more successfully into their performance.
Procedure	1. In the first or second meeting of the module, the tutor informs students of the assessment tasks and the assessment criteria.
	2. The tutor suggests a tentative outline with dates and activities that students will be following in each of the preparation sessions.
	3. In the third meeting, the tutor asks each student to nominate a topic in which he or she may be interested and could present to the class. The tutor groups students of similar interest together into groups of four.
	4. From the fourth to the eighth meeting, students brainstorm within their groups the sub-topics of their presentation. During the meetings, the tutor gives oral feedback on the sub-topics and gives suggestions for data/information collection.
	5. In the ninth meeting, each student presents part of his or her presentation. The tutor elicits feedback from peers to enable fellow students to see the strengths and weaknesses of each other's work and gives feedback on the performance.

Processing and Acting on Feedback

6. Students revise their work and prepare for the final presentation.
7. The final presentation takes place in the tenth and last meeting with the students. Students in their different groups present their topic in front of the class. The oral presentation is graded by the tutor using criteria developed for the task for the purpose of final assessment.
8. The oral presentation feedback form is used by the tutor and peers in giving feedback to the students during trial runs of their presentations as mentioned in point 5.

Supporting materials	☐	Oral presentation feedback form (Appendix).
Outcomes worth noting	☐	The feedback cycles integrate formative assessment into the module assignment in that what students learn in the process helps them in the final, summative assessment. This provides a strong motivation for taking feedback seriously.
Student response	☐	"We have divided our work early in the module and have done many rehearsals. We give comments to each other and have improved on our work a few times before the final presentation."
	☐	"I should interact more with the audience by asking their opinions. It helps them to engage in my topic."
	☐	"Tutor feedback is useful in pointing out my pronunciation mistakes."
How this practice supports learning	•	Oral assessment in the form of class presentations makes students' work 'public'. Hearing others' work helps students develop a sense of standards that should apply to their own work.
	•	Oral presentations can encourage students to prepare well, since their work will be critiqued by their peers.
	•	The provision of peer feedback also requires students to come to grips with standards and criteria as they prepare their comments for their fellow students.
	•	Feedback is provided in a timely way — students are able to use it in preparing their final presentation.
	•	This practice also encourages students to work on their assessment over time.
Further suggestions	•	Some, perhaps most, of the students' preparation could be done outside class time. They could send their emerging ideas to the tutor for comment.
	•	Students could practise giving feedback to one another in a briefing session in which a video of a presentation is shown.

Processing and Acting on Feedback

Contributor
Ina SIU
Department of English
The Hong Kong Institute of Education
Email: ina@ied.edu.hk

APPENDIX

Oral Presentation Feedback Form

Name of tutor/peer observer:

Name of student:

Topic of presentation:

Item	Fair	Good	Excellent
Clarity of aims			
Clarity of organization			
Use of voice			
Use of facial expressions/gestures			
Use of visual aids			
Grammaticality of speech			
Pronunciation, stress and rhythm			
Responding to the audience			
Team work			

Other comments:

Processing and Acting on Feedback

39. Using a professional development progress map to assess field experience

Sylvia Yee Fan TANG, The Hong Kong Institute of Education

Summary
The Professional Development Progress Map is a frame of reference against which a student's progress and achievement is mapped and monitored over time and used as an aid for the communication of feedback between the supervisor and student. To promote professional learning, the Progress Map can be used in the communication of evidence-based judgement and setting targets for improvement.

Situations where this practice could be used
Professional Development Progress Maps can be used in any form of professional practice where students' development in a number of areas of performance is expected to occur over a period of time. Such Progress Maps are developed at the programme level rather than at the level of the individual course or module.

Background	The use of the Professional Development Progress Map has been piloted in a range of in-service teacher education programmes run by the Hong Kong Institute of Education.
Rationale	□ Progress maps describe the knowledge, skills, understandings, attitudes, and values that a student is expected to develop over the period of their study. It provides a frame of reference against which progress and achievement can be mapped and monitored over time.
	□ The Progress Map can be used to chart professional development in different phases of field experience during the course of the student's programme. This facilitates *assessment for learning* as the level descriptors can be used as a reference for providing feedback to students about their strengths and weaknesses in different domains of practice. The level descriptors also make possible the setting of targets and priorities for professional development.
	□ The Progress Map can also be used for the purpose of *assessment of learning* — to show students' levels of attainment at different points of time.
Procedure	1. The supervisor conducts a pre-lesson conference with the student.
	2. The supervisor observes a lesson taught by the student.
	3. A post-lesson conference is held between the supervisor and the student. The professional dialogue between them involves communication about the student's professional development with

Processing and Acting on Feedback

regard to the Progress Map. Multiple sources of evidence, for example performance in the lesson observed, teaching artefacts and evidence of teacher collaboration, can be referred to in the communication.

4. The supervisor makes use of the Field Experience Feedback Form to take note of evidence of the student's achievements and to set targets with the student. The supervisor also works with the student to make judgment of and then chart the latter's levels of professional development in different domains on the Progress Map. Over time, the Progress Map can be used to plan the student's learning path.

Supporting materials	☐	The Professional Development Progress Map (Appendix 1) and a set of level descriptors for the different domains of teaching.
	☐	The Field Experience Feedback Form (Appendix 2).
Outcomes worth noting	☐	Active learner participation in the assessment process, rather than the instrumentation *per se*, is critical to the enhancement of professional learning.
	☐	Some students have made use of the Progress Map as a reference for assessing their own professional development — developing a sense of 'where they are' in the journey to fuller professional maturity.
	☐	There are a variety of ways of making explicit reference to the Progress Map in post-lesson conferences between the teaching supervisor and the teacher candidate.
	☐	The use of the Progress Map to support students' professional learning requires the presence of facilitating conditions, including teaching supervisors' and students' clear understanding of the Progress Map, their shared interpretation of the importance of active learner participation in the assessment process, adequate time for post-lesson conferencing, ample time for students' reflection, and manageable workloads on the part of teaching supervisors.
Student response	☐	"After I wrote my lesson plan, I checked my level of professional development. With reference to the level descriptors, I could also check whether I could make further improvement."
	☐	"With reference to the Progress Map, I had a general picture of my own performance. The Feedback Form was completed as a result of the two-way communication between the teaching supervisor and me. In the process of this two-way communication, I noticed my strengths, weaknesses and areas to be improved."
	☐	"*Involvement in education community* is important to a profession. ... Yet it is not related to the lesson observed ... . It should be assessed in other ways."

Processing and Acting on Feedback

How this practice supports learning	• Progress maps are particularly appropriate tools for involving students in the assessment and learning process since they:
	– set out the domain of a subject or area of professional practice in a comprehensive way;
	– describe different levels of performance that are expected at stages of a student's development; and
	– make this information available to all who are involved in the assessment and development process.
	• Progress maps provide an 'objective' basis for discussion, self and supervisor assessment, and setting targets for ongoing development.
	• Progress maps require considerable time and effort to develop and typically require input from a wide range of staff across a whole degree programme. However, once they are developed, they can be powerful instruments for assessment for all involved in a programme, and can be used for the duration of the programme.

Further suggestions	• Progress maps can be used at the beginning of field experience to identify student strengths and weaknesses and to plan appropriate learning experiences.
	• Progress maps can be tools for self-assessment or joint assessment between student and supervisor. Students can use them to identify their progress in different areas as a basis for discussion with their supervisor.
	• In classroom sessions, students could review each other's progress maps and provide constructive and formative commentaries, to improve understanding of the process.

Reference

Tang, S. Y. F., Cheng, M. M. H., and So, W. W. M. (2006) Supporting student teachers' professional learning with standards–referenced assessment. *Asia-Pacific Journal of Teacher Education*, 34, 2, 223–44.

Contributor

Sylvia Yee Fan TANG
Department of Educational Policy and Administration
The Hong Kong Institute of Education
Email: stang@ied.edu.hk

The contributor would like to acknowledge the colleagues at the Hong Kong Institute of Education who participated in the project 'Field Experience Assessment: The Professional Development Progress Map' funded by the HKIEd Projects and Initiatives Fund.

Processing and Acting on Feedback

APPENDIX 1

Field Experience Professional Development Progress Map

Programme: _____ Subject: _____ Participant's name: _____

Domain of teaching \ Level of development	Beginning	Threshold	Advanced Novice	Competent
1. Professional Attributes - Commitment and dedication to teaching - Passion for continuous learning				
2. Teaching and Learning — Understanding and organizing subject matter/content for student learning				
Planning instruction and designing learning experiences for all students				
Creating and maintaining effective environments for student learning				
Engaging and supporting all students to maximize their learning				
Assessing student learning and feedback				
3. Involvement in Education Community				

Programme year	Date of supervision	Supervisor's name	Supervisor's signature	Participant's signature
_____	_____	_____	_____	_____
_____	_____	_____	_____	_____
_____	_____	_____	_____	_____
_____	_____	_____	_____	_____
_____	_____	_____	_____	_____

Processing and Acting on Feedback

APPENDIX 2

Field Experience Feedback Form		
Participant's name:	Time:	
Programme year:	Class:	
Date:	Subject:	
School:	Topic:	
Domain of teaching	Evidence	Target for improvement
1. **Professional Attributes** – Commitment and dedication to teaching – Passion for continuous learning		
2. **Teaching and Learning** – Understanding and organizing subject matter/content for student learning – Planning instruction and designing learning experiences for all students – Creating and maintaining effective environments for student learning – Engaging and supporting all students to maximize their learning – Assessing student learning and feedback		
3. **Involvement in Education Community**		

4
The Way Forward

This concluding chapter addresses four main issues that are central to ongoing progress in reconfiguring assessment productively. Firstly, we look at some of the shifts in assessment in higher education in Hong Kong. Secondly, we return to some of the main challenges in assessment first raised in Chapter 1 and indicate how they might be tackled. Thirdly, we look at assessment at a macro-level and discuss some of the factors which inhibit assessment change and development. We propose a number of strategies which may be used to meet the identified constraints. Fourthly, we summarize some of the main implications for practice arising from our framework of learning-oriented assessment and the techniques in Chapter 3.

Identifiable shifts

Our wider experience in the Learning-oriented Assessment Project (LOAP) and our specific work on this book has enabled us to gauge some of the trends in assessment and to identify some shifts in thinking.

Assessment as a learning tool

Trends in the Hong Kong educational system across sectors are leading to a greater recognition of the potential of assessment as a learning tool. At the school level, for example, the education reform launched in 2001 promotes more diversified teaching and learning strategies, assessment for learning, learning-to-learn and a reduction in tests and examinations. The associated restructuring and renaming of the Hong Kong Examinations and Assessment Authority also points to a realization that testing is not the only way to evaluate student performance. The expansion of school-based assessment, although not without challenges, is also part of the development of greater diversity in assessment practices. This provides educators in Hong Kong with extensive opportunities to bring about meaningful and productive change to assessment.

At the university level, there is evidence of increased attention to the learning potential of assessment. Many initiatives are of an individual nature as illustrated in Chapter 3. The lessons from this book are that there is much good practice being carried out at this level without any additional funding or resource support. Good user-friendly practices should not be resource-intensive. The value in making these practices public through the publication of this book is to enable colleagues to consider how far these approaches are transferable to their particular context, and how much customization the practices would need to work in their own disciplines.

Outcomes-based approaches

What changes in university approaches to assessment are taking place? A prevailing trend is the development of outcomes-based education and associated assessment. Outcomes-based education is not a panacea but it seems to be a move in a useful direction. Outcomes statements concentrate on the outputs rather than the inputs of teaching. This aligns well with the focus of this book on how the process of learning can support the development of enhanced student performance. A relevant feature of an outcomes-based approach might be more diversified modes of assessment, including performance assessments that allow us to obtain a more holistic view of student progress towards stated learning outcomes. Challenges for outcomes-based approaches include the difficulty of assessing generic outcomes on a programme-wide level (Maki, 2004); identifying worthwhile outcomes that capture the essence of learning without being too narrow; catering for important but unintended emergent learning outcomes (Hussey and Smith, 2003) and avoiding the risk of accountability and bureaucratization overshadowing a focus on what really matters, namely student learning (Tavner, 2005). Despite these concerns learning outcomes do carry the potential to contribute to the kind of constructive alignment through assessment tasks as learning tasks illustrated in Chapter 3. When learning outcomes are worthwhile and clearly stated, and assessment tasks require students to work productively towards these outcomes, then students are being primed for deep learning experiences.

Alternative assessment

As part of the growing interest in alternative forms of assessment, we also identify evidence of students being increasingly exposed to less traditional modes of assessment. Our belief is that students are largely responding positively to a greater range of assessment methods, provided they can see their learning benefits. International experiences of introducing innovative assessment (e.g. McDowell and Sambell, 1999) suggest that with good preparation and rehearsal opportunities students can benefit considerably from innovative assessment, but there can be teething troubles in the early stages. Vitally important is the need to explain why an assessment method is being used and how students will gain. As with all innovations, users need to see how it will benefit them.

Approaches within the peer assessment/peer learning nexus are clearly now in the repertoire of large numbers of tutors in Hong Kong and numerous examples of this are seen in Chapter 3. There is also an increasing body of local literature related to peer assessment e.g. Cheng and Warren (2000, 2003); Lopez-Real and Chan (1999); MacAlpine (1999); and Sivan (2000). Involving peers in assessment has potential to increase learner independence, raise standards and reduce tutor marking load (e.g. Liu and Carless, 2006). A further advantage is that Hong Kong students are generally well-disposed to working in groups and they sometimes initiate their own peer learning groups, independently of the tutor, thereby increasing learning time and reducing reliance on the tutor.

Technology-enhanced assessment

A further, highly predictable, shift is the increasing use of technology to enhance teaching, learning and assessment. Online management systems, such as Blackboard, are popular ways of managing resources, facilitating learner autonomy and developing collegial patterns of work. Assessment has the potential to drive this collaborative online process. One of the strengths of learning management systems is that they provide communication tools to foster and enhance peer learning by facilitating easy access to the opinions of other students. A further advantage is that they may support efficient provision of prompt feedback to students. These processes can facilitate the development of quality assignments enhanced through feedback and revision. Technology can also facilitate a wider repertoire of assessment methods, including electronic portfolios, online assessment and automated feedback.

Meeting the challenges of assessment

In Chapter 1, we outlined some of the main challenges to the enhancement of assessment practice. We now return to these issues and suggest how they might be tackled. We do this through drawing on the techniques discussed in this book, the wider work of LOAP and relevant literature in Hong Kong and overseas. We address six themes: double duty, examinations, criterion-referenced assessment, feedback, assessing group work and plagiarism.

Double duty

We introduced in Chapter 1, Boud's concept of double duty: assessments need to do a number of things simultaneously. That assessments need to lead to both the award of a reliable grade and contribute to productive student learning is a tension facing tutors. The learning-oriented approach to assessment espoused in this book is indicative of our belief that the formative aspects of assessment need to be strengthened in the ways outlined in Chapter 2. The dominance of the summative paradigm, however, indicates that we need to seek productive synergies between formative and summative. One strategy is the integration of formative processes within a summative assignment in the ways illustrated in Chapter 3, for example in techniques 16 and 36. Another complementary strategy is the design of effective summative assignments which support the development of desired learning outcomes by pushing students to use deep learning processes, for example, techniques 6 and 26.

Examinations

Examinations are a useful tool and carry a number of advantages in terms of being well-recognized, free from plagiarism and generally perceived as fair. They are valuable as part of a diet of mixed assessment methods and are usually considered reasonably straightforward to set and administer, although they normally have little or no formative function. We believe that examinations are most useful in combination with other methods — they need to be supplemented by other assessment tasks which can probe skills that examinations are unlikely to gauge. The techniques in this collection exemplify the range of assessment strategies which may be complementary or alternative to examinations, for example, project-based assessment (techniques 18, 22 and 29); portfolio assessment (technique 27); and critical incident analysis (technique 4). Technique 26 also discusses how a test was modified to encourage deeper learning amongst students.

Criterion-referenced assessment and standards

Criterion-referenced assessment makes performance standards clear and transparent to both students and staff. Criterion-referenced assessment integrates well with learning-oriented assessment and outcomes-based education because students can be prompted to self-evaluate their progress towards the stated criteria. They know the intended outcomes and strive to progress towards them.

Through this process, it is our belief that learning-oriented assessment can enhance student performance and so lead to higher standards and better grades for students. This is a key advantage both for students and lecturers of this kind of orientation towards assessment. The enhancement of standards can be achieved by challenging assessment tasks calibrated against clearly stated criteria. Increasing students' awareness of quality work also enhances their engagement with these standards and criteria.

Feedback and marking loads

Feedback to students is both an essential aspect of the tutor role and a challenge to handle efficiently when faced with large class sizes and modularized courses. The use of technology is one strategy for communicating with a large cohort. For example, in technique 6, a model answer is posted on the course web site allowing a large class to receive prompt feedback on a set problem. Techniques 12 and 13 use automated feedback which carries potential for workload efficiency and use by large numbers of students. Internationally, many are arguing that the extensive use of computer-assisted feedback is likely to be highly beneficial to students when it is integral to the learning process (Juwah et al., 2004).

Assessing group work

Assessing group work has positive impacts on student learning but can be a challenge in providing reliable individual grades. It is worth reiterating some of the key advantages of group work: it facilitates peer learning; it stimulates key generic skills, such as teamwork and communication skills; and it can reduce the tutor marking workload. There are strategies for ensuring that students are awarded fair grades (see Kuisma, 1998, for a useful summary). Group assignments should not be overused and in particular it is usually inadvisable for a group assignment to be the only assessment for a module. They can, however, serve as an effective component of varied suites of assessments which promote different learning and different skills. Group processes are highlighted, for example, in techniques 3, 8, 18, 21 and 22.

Plagiarism

Plagiarism is not a new problem in higher education, but it is one that currently is gaining increasing attention internationally (Carroll, 2005). How tasks are set can facilitate or discourage plagiarism, for example setting the same question every year obviously invites plagiarism. Strategies to reduce or discourage plagiarism include: the involvement of students and lecturers in the preparatory and developmental stages of assessments; in-class time being used to report and review progress on assignments; and students submitting work incrementally as exemplified in technique 37. In short, the more students and lecturers are involved co-operatively in the assessment processes, the less likely it is that plagiarism will occur. Plagiarism is explicitly addressed in technique 1 and also discouraged by many other techniques, especially those which include tutor or peer critique of work in progress.

Tackling assessment issues that inhibit student learning

We now turn to a more macro-level and discuss potentially inhibiting factors to the adoption of a learning-oriented approach to assessment. These are discussed below with some strategies for tackling them outlined.

Factor 1   Dominance of assessment as grading

A major challenge to learning-oriented assessment is the dominance of the notion of assessment as grading. There is a danger that Hong Kong students spend too much time being tested, and not enough time in productive learning. As a consequence, if students (and/or their tutors) see assessment as work in exchange for grades, why would they be interested in a learning-oriented perspective on assessment?

We believe that this point of view discredits our students. Learning is much more than the accumulation of grades. The majority of university students actually want motivating assessment activities which involve them in productive learning experiences. And of course, they want high grades, too! Under a constructively aligned system, well-articulated assessment tasks will demand strong student learning outcomes in order for students to obtain high grades.

It is also our contention that, from a more pragmatic perspective, a learning-oriented approach is not incompatible with seeing assessment as a 'performance for grades' exchange. We believe that a learning-oriented approach to assessment is likely to lead to better student grades because it involves students actively in the assessment, engages them with standards and encourages them to monitor and improve their own work. This may lead to higher levels of student satisfaction and hence tutors obtaining better results in student evaluations of teaching. Learning-oriented assessment thus has the potential to provide a win–win situation for both tutors and students.

Factor 2   The challenge of tutor time and workload

Academics are perennially busy and faced with multiple pressures to produce tangible products of various kinds. There is a certain labour-intensiveness to some of the good practices described in this book. The pressures of time and workload have to be acknowledged and there are no easy solutions to these challenges. Is there anything that can be done to soften these pressures?

Collaborative approaches to assessment carry potential to share the challenges of workload. Tutors can share ideas, strategies, worksheets, model answers, quality exemplars or follow-up tasks as part of the process of streamlining assessment. Less reinvention of the wheel and more sharing of good practices can also play a role. Part of the motivation for this book is to provide a convenient means of sharing techniques and associated materials.

We also speculate as to whether there is a case for a reduction in the amount of detail provided in comments on summative assignments and this case may be particularly strong with respect to final year students. We have argued in Chapters 1 and 2 that much feedback is largely ineffective because of the lack of timeliness and the lack of opportunity for students to act on the feedback. As that is the case, why do we spend so much time writing detailed comments that students may not engage with? Of course, students are entitled to receive comments on their work, but might these be reconfigured as one or two key points for further development? Further investigation into effective and user-friendly ways of providing written feedback on summative assignments would be particularly useful.

Factor 3   *The challenge of student time and workload*

Students are also often under pressure. They are naturally interested in marks, so may be sceptical about tasks that do not carry an immediate grading reward. What does learning-oriented assessment offer to students?

We believe that learning-oriented assessment is most persuasive when it is used in association with summative assessment, in other words, when the techniques used help students to do good work, achieve stated learning outcomes and get good grades in assignments. Many of the techniques in this book have illustrated this, e.g. feedback and reflections on work in progress; or peer and self-assessment processes that enable misconceptions to be ironed out before submission of the final product. In other words, the technique directly supports enhanced performance in summative assessment.

We also believe that students can be motivated to do worthwhile tasks that do not carry marks, although this may represent more of a challenge. Such tasks can be done in class without adding to student workload. They can also be successfully done out of class when students are able to identify how the task helps them to learn better (and hence get higher marks), how the task fits in with a future assessed task, or simply that the task is interesting, worthwhile and stimulating for its own sake, irrespective of its relationship with summative assessment.

Factor 4   *Lack of deep understanding of assessment issues*

An issue that we became increasingly aware of during the process of the LOAP project was that staff understanding of key issues in assessment varies enormously. Within a single institution this understanding may range from a high degree of expertise to major misconceptions about crucial issues. A lack of understanding of assessment is a barrier to ongoing improvement and can impact negatively on students.

Is there any evidence of development of tutor knowledge of assessment and its implications? In recent years, a number of initiatives and projects related to assessment have been carried out within the Hong Kong context. One of the main foci of the second round of the Teaching and Learning Quality Process Reviews (TLQPR) was on assessment. This process mobilized many staff in universities in discussing assessment issues, collecting relevant documentation and defending their assessment processes in front of visiting panels. The University Grants Committee has compiled a collection of good practices emanating from this TLQPR exercise (UGC, 2005).

There have also been a number of large-scale staff development initiatives related to assessment. For example, in addition to LOAP, Hong Kong Polytechnic University has also carried out a three-year teaching development project entitled 'Enhancing Teaching and Learning through Assessment' (Hong Kong Polytechnic, 2006). By their nature, however, such staff development initiatives tend to attract the enthusiasts, those who are already cognizant of the issues in assessment and want to learn more. The improvement of practice amongst those who are less focused on the interplay between assessment and student learning is an ongoing challenge meriting further attention.

Factor 5   Staff attitudes

Only a small minority of university staff seem to be attracted to the topic of assessment. Perhaps assessment carries too many negative connotations: of unfairness in assessment; our own sometimes painful experiences of assessment; or the burden of marking that is an inevitable part of assessment processes. Assessment all too often is seen as drudgery with little reward, rather than as an important way to foster student learning. Assessment is in need of a public relations makeover.

How might one promote more positive attitudes towards assessment? Assessment needs to be seen as less of a technical issue, and more of a humanistic one that impacts on student learning. We are all interested in learning, so putting the learning more convincingly into assessment can be a positive step forward. Learning-oriented assessment plays a key role here in promoting assessment discourse firmly focused on student learning. More reporting of positive experiences and practices in how assessment can be co-opted to support learning can also contribute to this changed emphasis.

Even greater recognition may be required of how important assessment is to students. Students cannot proceed in their studies without effective assessment. From a pragmatic perspective, lecturers who want to teach successfully and get good student evaluations need to handle assessment processes skilfully so as to maximize student learning and associated satisfaction.

Factor 6   Lack of trust

Trust or mistrust imbue many life experiences, indeed, Fukuyama (1995) suggests we live in an era of distrust. Trust is essential to many elements of the assessment process. Some examples: peer assessment can be mistrusted when we do not have faith in students assessing seriously or fairly; group assessment prompts concerns about freeloaders; examinations may be preferred to assignments because we do not trust students not to cheat. In short, lack of trust can act as a constraint against alternative assessment methods. Sometimes our lack of trust in students may be justified, other times less so.

Students may not trust lecturers to grade fairly, suspecting favouritism. Colleagues or administrators may not trust lecturers to grade reliably; is the 'bell curve' spread of grades partly a response to lack of trust in staff grading practices? Are some staff thought to award generous marks so as to achieve better teaching evaluations from their students?

Certainly we cannot remove distrust from the assessment process but there are things that can be done to ameliorate matters. The most fundamental way of minimizing distrust is through transparency. The more open lecturers are about assessment procedures, what is required and how grades are awarded, the more comfortable students are likely to be. We also need to create a trusting climate in which students feel ready to admit their weaknesses and seek advice for the challenges that they face. Assessment dialogues in which students and lecturers discuss issues related to the assessment process as a general concept, but not related to the specifics of subject matter or what students need to do for a particular assignment (Carless, 2006), can be particularly useful in enhancing transparency and reducing distrust. An important aim is for students to start to understand assessment processes in a way approaching that of their lecturers.

Factor 7   *Institutional inertia or lack of commitment*

A number of respondents to the LOAP questionnaire survey (Liu, 2005) felt that institutional inertia or a lack of commitment to tackling problems in assessment was a barrier to change. In particular, whilst individual staff can make a difference, some issues need to be tackled at an institutional level. Mobilizing senior staff or middle management can be challenging when they are faced with multiple commitments in a highly pressurized working environment.

Strategies at the institutional level may include the following:

- using a combination of bottom-up processes to involve staff collegially and top-down impetus from management;
- collaborating with the educational development unit in the university;
- introducing an outcomes-based approach to the curriculum;
- valuing and disseminating experiences of staff who have experimented successfully with innovations in assessment;
- providing greater incentives and rewards for those achieving positive outcomes in teaching, learning and assessment;
- drawing in high calibre external input to provide cutting-edge thought and to benchmark practices against international norms; and
- building staff development for assessment around a series of academic or 'scholarship of teaching' products, so that the production of refereed output can be achieved.

Assessment strategies for enhanced learning

Turning now to a summary of recommended learning-oriented assessment strategies, we return to the three core components of our conceptual framework from Chapter 2.

Assessment tasks as learning tasks

- The assessment task is clearly one of the most important elements of the assessment process. Tasks should be aligned with curriculum objectives and content in a way that promotes productive learning.
- Assessment tasks should mirror the kind of learning we wish to promote. Complex learning outcomes require complex assessment tasks.
- Tasks should motivate students to produce their best performance.
- Assessment tasks should facilitate student involvement through self-monitoring and peer critique (see also student involvement below).
- Tasks should be sequenced and planned so that they facilitate feedback that is timely and can be acted upon (see also feedback below).

Student involvement in assessment

- Students should be involved as actively as possible in all aspects of assessment processes, from task design to the awarding of grades.
- Where feasible, students should be engaged in identifying, drafting, summarizing or using assessment criteria. These processes sensitize students to the required standards and provide the first step towards student self-monitoring of their own performance.
- Students also need to engage with quality exemplars. In association with the previous points, this can help to raise student awareness of standards and how their performance may differ from the exemplars.
- Dialogues with students about assessment processes can also facilitate transparency and enhance mutual trust.

Feedback as feedforward

- Feedback needs to be timely. Too often feedback in higher education comes after modules are completed and too late to be of much use to students. As tutors we may need to refigure our assignments, so that students can get earlier feedback and make better use of it.
- Feedback needs to be acted upon. We need to focus on ways to maximize the opportunities for students to act upon the feedback we are providing. Feedback on drafts, feedback that promotes self-monitoring, and 'quick and dirty' oral feedback are the kind of modes which are most forward-looking.

Concluding comments on learning-oriented assessment

One of the starting points of LOAP and the genesis of this book was an evolving conceptualization of learning-oriented assessment. We believe that, both conceptually and in terms of implications for practice, learning-oriented assessment makes a contribution to the scholarship of teaching, learning and assessment. We have conceptualized learning-oriented assessment as falling within the domain of assessment that focuses on learning (rather than on grading). We view learning-oriented assessment as comprising three main elements: assessment tasks as learning tasks; student involvement in assessment; and feedback as feedforward. The implementation of these elements is enhanced when students are working towards clearly stated learning outcomes, aligned with module content and assessments.

The techniques in Chapter 3 are congruent with this framework and showcase how learning-oriented assessment can be put into practice in the university context. The techniques in Chapter 3 provide a stimulus for assessment change. They illustrate good practices in learning-oriented assessment in our universities and act as a catalyst for further experimentation and development. By adapting selected techniques to our own disciplinary or contextual needs, further progress is within our grasp. We identify a key way forward as developing productive synergies between formative and summative assessment, an aspect of what is referred to as 'double duty'. Assessments that can support both productive learning as well as the grading function are those best suited to developing desired learning outcomes.

In conclusion, we hope that this book can enrich the reader's strategies in terms of the design of appropriate learning tasks, student involvement in assessment, and the provision of forward-looking feedback. We believe progress in assessment has been made, yet acknowledge that there is still much more to be done in view of the complex and multifaceted nature of assessment.

Appendix:
Useful Resources

This annotated list of web sites, journal articles and books is not meant to be an exhaustive guide to assessment resources and ideas in higher education. It is rather a selective choice of what we consider to be some of the best and most influential resources and ideas. We hope that most academics, regardless of their level of knowledge and philosophy of assessment, will find something of interest and relevance for their practice in these resources.

Web sites

1. The Higher Education Academy (2005). *Assessment*. Retrieved 26 April 2006, from http://www.heacademy.ac.uk/resources.asp?process=filter_fields&section=generic&type=some&id=1

   Funded in the UK, and hosting a diversity of materials produced by its predecessor organizations (the Institute for Learning and Teaching in Higher Education and the Learning and Teaching Support Network), the Higher Education Academy site has many downloadable documents in its 'Resources' database. They cover a variety of assessment methods (e.g., portfolio, problem-based, work-based, peer and self-assessment) and guidelines for assessing large classes and preventing plagiarism. Feedback is featured in a 44-page booklet on 'Enhancing student learning through effective formative feedback', a useful resource that includes case studies in various disciplines and different techniques for giving effective feedback (e.g., using an electronic voting system for immediate feedback in interactive lectures). A six-page 'Assessment criteria grid' contains thirty-five criteria and descriptors that could be adopted or adapted for assessment in various disciplines. There are also useful generic assessment guides for lecturers, senior managers, heads of department and students.

2.   Centre for the Study of Higher Education, The University of Melbourne (2005). *Assessing Learning in Australian Universities*. Retrieved 26 April 2006, from http://www.cshe.unimelb. edu.au/assessinglearning/08/index.html

Two sections in this University of Melbourne site are especially useful for academics interested in finding solutions to their own assessment problems and challenges. The first is the 'Good practice directory', which contains tried and tested techniques by academics in different disciplines. Examples include open book examinations in Veterinary Science, randomized online assessment in Mathematics and Statistics and assessing pre-laboratory work in Chemistry.

The other particularly practical part is a 'Ready-to-use resources' section that contains numerous ideas for assessment. These include strategies for online assessment, group work assessment and assessment of large classes. Academics would also find something useful among the thirty-six strategies for minimizing plagiarism (e.g. asking students to include the call number of each paper source they used and the date they accessed each web site; asking students to supply photocopies of any references used as part of an appendix; and designing assessment tasks that provide little or no opportunities for plagiarism).

3.   Teaching and Educational Development Institute, University of Queensland (2005). *Assessment*. Retrieved 26 April 2006, from http://www.tedi.uq.edu.au/teaching/assessment/ index.html

This University of Queensland site contains good guidelines and examples of macro-planning for assessment. Topics such as 'Designing assessment programmes' and 'Learning goals and graduate attributes' contextualize assessment at the programme and institutional levels. It also discusses assessment issues that concern most academics, e.g., grades and feedback and group assessment.

4.   Institute for Interactive Media and Learning, University of Technology, Sydney (2005). *Assessment*. Retrieved 26 April 2006, from http://www.iml.uts.edu.au/assessment/

This University of Technology, Sydney site should be useful for academics who want a brief guide to some essentials in assessment. It contains sections on formative feedback, streamlining marking, preventing plagiarism, and involving students in assessment. The guidelines may be somewhat general for academics who are looking for specific solutions or ideas for their assessment problems. The section on preventing plagiarism is also useful.

5.   Computer Assisted Assessment Centre (2005). *Resources*. Retrieved 26 April 2006, from http: //www.caacentre.ac.uk/resources/index.shtml

This Computer Assisted Assessment (CAA) Centre site provides a wealth of subject-specific and general resources for CAA. It also includes case studies and software reviews. The latter could become out-of-date as the site is the product of a UK project that ended in 2002. However, the CAA conference site at http://www.caaconference.com/ provides conference proceedings for the last nine years of the UK Computer Assisted Assessment Conference, which develops the work of many of the people associated with the original UK Fund for the Development of Teaching and Learning (FDTL) project.

6. CIAD Centre for Interactive Assessment Development (2005) Retrieved 26 April 2006, from http://www.derby.ac.uk/ciad/dev/links.html

This site contains a number of resources within the theme of computer-based assessment. Links are organized within the following sub-themes:

- Introduction to computer-based assessment
- CAA organizations
- CAA case studies
- Assessment texts and publications
- Item analysis software information
- Question design resources

The site is suitable for both newcomers to CAA and more experienced practitioners.

Journal articles and books

1. Black, P. and Wiliam, D. (1998) Inside the black box: Raising standards through classroom assessment. *Phi Delta Kappan*, 80(2), 139–148.

This paper represents the shortened version of the classic 67-page meta-analysis of research on formative assessment (Black and Wiliam, 1998). The authors make a convincing case for the effectiveness of formative assessment in all educational settings across all sectors of education. The role of self-assessment is highlighted as a crucial component of formative approaches to assessment. Policy and implementation issues are also discussed.

2. Boud, D. (2000) Sustainable assessment: Rethinking assessment for the learning society. *Studies in Continuing Education, 22*(2), 151–167.

Boud argues that the purposes of assessment should be extended to include the preparation of students for lifelong learning. He refers to this concept as sustainable assessment, a form of assessment which meets not only the specific and immediate goals of a course, but also incorporates the knowledge, skills and predispositions needed for effective lifelong learning and assessments in the future. Similar arguments are also developed further in Boud and Falchikov (2006).

3. Boud, D., Cohen, R. and Sampson J. (1999) Peer learning and assessment. *Assessment and Evaluation in Higher Education, 24*(4), 413–426.

This paper examines the use of assessment methods that foster collaborative peer learning. These include group assessment, peer feedback, self-assessment, assessment of participation and negotiated assessment. It concludes with a discussion of the assessment issues related to peer learning that require further investigation.

4. Elton, L. and Johnston, B. (2002) *Assessment in Universities: A Critical Review of Research*. UK: The Higher Education Academy.

A 110-page review aimed at academics who want to improve practice within current assessment methods or change current assessment methods. The two main chapters are focused on 'challenges to established practice' and 'some basic assessment dilemmas with particular reference to portfolios'. The latter reviews the use of portfolio assessment in a range of disciplines.

5. Gibbs, G. and Simpson, C. (2004) Conditions under which assessment supports students' learning. *Learning and Teaching in Higher Education*, 1, 3–31.

This paper focuses on two critical aspects in assessment. The first is the way assessment affects student learning out of class. The second is assessment feedback and how it can improve learning. It reviews the literature in these two areas and proposes eleven conditions under which assessment supports enhanced learning. These conditions offer a practical framework for academics to review their own assessment practice. We have drawn on this framework in constructing our conceptual framework in Chapter 2.

6. Knight, P. (2002) Summative assessment in higher education: Practices in disarray. *Studies in Higher Education*, 27(3), 275–286.

Knight critiques current practices in high stakes assessment and questions their validity and reliability. He argues for 'a release from expensive attempts to do the impossible', i.e., summative assessment cannot deliver the precision and certainty that common sense expects, at least not at a price that higher education institutions can afford. He argues in favour of a re-appraisal of assessment as a complex system of sense-making and claims making. This means 'placing psychometrics under erasure while revaluing assessment practices as primarily communicative practices'.

7. Sadler, D. R. (1989) Formative assessment and the design of instructional systems. *Instructional Science*, 18, 119–144.

In this seminal article, Sadler argues that feedback as commonly defined in terms of information given to the student about the quality of performance is too narrow to be of much use. He identifies three necessary conditions that must be satisfied simultaneously for effective feedback. The learner has to progressively acquire a concept of the standard being aimed for, develop the capacity to compare the current level of performance with the standard, and develop a repertoire of strategies which can be drawn upon to improve her own work. The acquisition of this tacit 'evaluative expertise' cannot take place through understanding descriptive statements of standard and exemplars alone, it requires prolonged engagement in authentic evaluative activity guided by the teacher.

8. Yorke, M. (2003) Formative assessment in higher education: Moves towards theory and the enhancement of pedagogic practice. *Higher Education*, 45, 477–501.

Yorke sketches the theoretical development of formative assessment and argues that a theory of formative assessment needs to include, amongst other things, disciplinary epistemology, students' stages of intellectual development and the psychology of giving and receiving feedback. He argues that the feedback process, though essential to formative assessment, may inhibit learning when it encourages learner dependence. Research into formative assessment is discussed and suggestions are made regarding a research agenda that may contribute to the improvement of pedagogy.

9. Falchikov, N. (2005) *Improving Assessment through Student Involvement: Practical Solutions for Aiding Learning in Higher and Further Education.* London and New York: Routledge.

In this detailed yet accessible text, Falchikov focuses on student involvement in assessment, particularly through peer assessment and self-assessment. She unpacks some of the problems in carrying out these forms of assessment and explores a number of strategies which minimize these challenges. The book is a rich resource of findings across numerous disciplines and the detailed references provide a comprehensive testament to the range of research and practices related to the theme of student involvement in assessment.

10. Carless, D., Joughin, G., and Mok, M. M. C. (Eds.) (2006) Learning-oriented assessment: Principles and practice. *Assessment and Evaluation in Higher Education,* Volume 31(4).

This special issue showcases some of the work related to learning-oriented assessment carried out by LOAP and its overseas consultants. The contributions in the issue are as follows:

Carless, D., Joughin, G. and Mok, M.M.C. Learning-oriented assessment: Principles and practice, 395–8.

Boud, D. and Falchikov, N. Aligning assessment with long-term learning, 399–413.

Mok, M., Lung, C. L., Cheng, P. W., Cheung, H. P., and Ng, M. L. Self-assessment in higher education: Experience in using a metacognitive approach in five case studies, 415–33.

Knight, P. The local practices of assessment, 435–52.

Keppell, M., Au, E., Ma, A. and Chan, C. Peer learning and learning-oriented assessment in technology-enhanced environments, 453–64.

Russell, J., Elton, L., Swinglehurst, D. and Greenhalgh, T. Using e-learning in assessment for learning: A case study of a web-based course in primary care, 465–78.

Other sources of practical advice

1. Habeshaw, S., Gibbs, G., and Habeshaw, T. (1993) *53 Interesting Ways to Assess Your Students.* Bristol: Technical and Educational Services.

The purpose of this book is to describe a wide range of ways of assessing students. The book is divided into ten main chapters as follows: essays, objective tests, computer-based assessment, exams, on-the-spot assessment (vivas, exhibitions and observations), assessment over time (diaries or log books, portfolios and archives, i.e. asking students to start building up an archive of their assessed work and comparing their earlier efforts with more recent achievements), assessing projects and practicals, criteria, feedback to students, and involving students in the assessment process. The final chapter is entitled 'issues in assessment' and discusses five issues: choosing assessment methods, weighting, degree classifications, pass/fail assessment, and gender bias. Although there is no conceptual framework to bind the collection together, this book is a useful source of ideas for teachers in higher education interested in diversifying their practices or finding fresh ideas on a specific assessment area.

2. Hounsell, D., McCulloch, M., and Scott, M. (1996) *The ASSHE Inventory: Changing Assessment Practices in Scottish Higher Education.* Edinburgh: Centre for Teaching, Learning and Assessment, The University of Edinburgh and Napier University.

ASSHE (Assessment Strategies in Scottish Higher Education) was a two-year survey and dissemination project carried out in the mid-1990s. It has been highly influential, especially in the UK. Around one hundred entries, selected from a database of more than three hundred, are included in the collection. The contributors are drawn from a wide range of disciplines and institutions. Each entry represents a change in assessment practice and explores what prompted the change. One of the potential uses of the inventory is to look at different ways that colleagues respond to assessment challenges and consider what might be entailed if one were to modify one's own practices in a similar fashion. The collection can also be accessed in its web format via the Higher Education Academy web site: http://www.heacademy.ac.uk/resources.asp?process= full_record&section=generic&id=14

3. Nightingale, P., Te Wiata, I., Toohey, S., Ryan, G., Hughes, C., and Magin, D. (1996) *Assessing Learning in Universities.* Sydney: University of New South Wales Press.

This is a rich and detailed text of more than three hundred pages, derived from a project carried out in the mid-1990s at the University of New South Wales. The overall aim was to produce a series of user-friendly materials of practical assistance in assessing and examining in a wide range of disciplinary areas. The emphasis of the project was on student learning outcomes and was grouped around eight clusters of abilities: thinking critically and making judgements, solving problems and developing plans, performing procedures and demonstrating techniques, managing and developing oneself, accessing and managing information, demonstrating knowledge and understanding, designing, creating, performing, and communicating. Case study materials are developed within each theme and are presented in the following format: context, abilities being assessed, assessment procedure, criteria for assessment, strengths and limitations, and comment. This insightful collection is both detailed and user-friendly and has influenced the development of our collection of Hong Kong-based practices.

4. Dunn, L., Morgan, C., O'Reilly, M., and Parry S. (2004) *The Student Assessment Handbook: New Directions in Traditional and Online Assessment.* Abingdon: Routledge.

The first part of the book is a highly accessible yet scholarly introduction to contemporary issues in assessment that makes reference to established generic texts on assessment but puts a new spin on them. The second part focuses on 'fitness-for-purpose' i.e. the selection of the best methods and approaches for the context, the subject, the level and the student body. A particularly helpful feature of this section is the extensive use of illustrative case studies. The third part of the book, looking at assessment in practice, is linked to design issues in a way that encourages constructive alignment. The centrality of the student experience to assessment is emphasized here, especially the need for students to understand fully the process and the reasons behind it, which we know can dramatically impact on student retention and achievement if undertaken properly.

5.   Brown, S. and Glasner, A. (Eds.) (1999) *Assessment Matters in Higher Education: Choosing and Using Diverse Approaches*. Buckingham: Open University Press.

This edited collection includes work from a range of distinguished scholars on broad assessment topics including systems approaches to assessment, exploring the effectiveness of innovative assessment, assessing practice and fostering autonomous assessment. It provides both theoretical perspectives and pragmatic advice on how to conduct effective assessment. The chapters on innovative approaches and helping students to understand the processes of self and peer assessment are particularly useful.

6.   Schwartz, P. and Webb, G. (Eds.) (2002) *Assessment: Case Studies, Experience and Practice from Higher Education*. London: Kogan Page.

This accessible book brings together a wide range of international assessment case studies, illustrating how a variety of academics have dealt with issues associated with information technology and assessment, reflective assessment techniques, institution-wide assessment, assessment methods for problem-based learning and short intensive courses. Each case is accompanied by sections asking, 'What is going on here? What factors have contributed to the situation described? How does the case reporter see the situation? What other interpretations might there be? How might the situation have been handled? What general issues are brought out by the case? What are its generic lessons for readers and others?'. The editors encourage readers to read each case and 'play the game' by noting their own impressions before going on to find out how the protagonists acted in reality and thinking through how else it could have been dealt with.

References

Biggs, J. (1996) Review and recommendations. In J. Biggs (Ed.), *Testing: To Educate or Select? Education in Hong Kong at the Crossroads*. Hong Kong: Hong Kong Educational Publishing.

Biggs, J. (2003) *Teaching for Quality Learning at University* (second edition). Maidenhead: Open University Press/SRHE.

Black, P. and Wiliam, D. (1998) Assessment and classroom learning, *Assessment in Education*, 5(1), 7–74.

Boud, D. (1991) *Implementing Student Self-Assessment*. Sydney: Higher Education Research and Development Society of Australasia.

Boud, D. (1995) *Enhancing Learning through Self-Assessment*. London: Kogan Page.

Boud, D. (2000) Sustainable assessment: Rethinking assessment for the learning society. *Studies in Continuing Education*, 22(2), 151–67.

Boud, D., Cohen, R. and Sampson, J. (Eds.) (2001) *Peer Learning in Higher Education: Learning from and with Each Other*. London: Routledge.

Boud, D. and Falchikov, N. (2006) Aligning assessment with long-term learning. *Assessment and Evaluation in Higher Education*, 31(4), 391–413.

Carless, D. (2006) Differing perceptions in the feedback process. *Studies in Higher Education*, 31(2), 219–33.

Carless, D., Joughin, G., and Mok, M. (2006) Learning-oriented assessment: Principles and practice. *Assessment and Evaluation in Higher Education*, 31(4), 395–98.

Carroll, J. (2005) *A Handbook for Deterring Plagiarism in Higher Education*. Oxford: Oxford Centre for Staff and Learning Development.

Cheng, W., and Warren, M. (2000) Making a difference: Using peers to assess individual students' contributions to a group project. *Teaching in Higher Education*, 5 (2) 243–55.

Cheng, W. and Warren, M. (2003) Having second thoughts: Student perceptions before and after a peer assessment exercise. In P. Stimpson, P. Morris, Y. Fung and R. Carr (Eds.) *Curriculum, Learning and Assessment: The Hong Kong Experience*. Hong Kong: Open University of Hong Kong Press.

Fukuyama, F. (1995) *Trust: Social Virtues and the Creation of Prosperity*. New York: Free Press.

Gibbs, G. and Simpson, C. (2004) Conditions under which assessment supports students' learning. *Learning and Teaching in Higher Education*, 1, 3–31.

Hong Kong Polytechnic (2006) Enhancing Teaching and Learning through Assessment. Retrieved 20 April 2006, from Assessment Resource Centre, http://www.polyu.edu.hk/assessment/arc/about/arc.htm

Higgins, R., Hartley, P., and Skelton, A. (2001) Getting the message across: The problem of communicating assessment feedback. *Teaching in Higher Education*, 6(2), 269–74.

Higgins, R., Hartley, P., and Skelton, A. (2002) The conscientious consumer: Reconsidering the role of assessment feedback in student learning. *Studies in Higher Education*, 27(1), 53–64.

Hussey, T. and Smith, P. (2003) The uses of learning outcomes. *Teaching in Higher Education*, 8(3), 357–68.

Johnson, V. (2003) *Grade Inflation: A Crisis in College Education*. New York: Springer.

Joughin, G. (2005) *Learning Oriented Assessment: A Conceptual Framework*. In G. Crebert, L. Davies and S. Phillips (Eds.), CD-ROM of *Conference Proceedings, Effective Teaching and Learning Conference*, Brisbane.

Juwah, C., Macfarlane-Dick, D., Mathews, B., Nicol, D., Ross, D. and Smith, B. (2004) *Enhancing Student Learning through Effective Formative Feedback*. York: Higher Education Academy.

Kuisma, R. (1998) Assessing individual contribution to a group project. In D. Watkins, C. Tang, J. Biggs and R. Kuisma (Eds.), *Assessment of University Students in Hong Kong: How and Why, Assessment Portfolio, Students' Grading*. Hong Kong: City University of Hong Kong.

Liu, N. F. (2005) *Hong Kong Academics' and Students' Perceptions of Assessment Purposes and Practices*. Learning Oriented Assessment Project Report: Hong Kong Institute of Education.

Liu, N. F. and Carless, D. (2006) Peer feedback: The learning element of peer assessment. *Teaching in Higher Education*, 11(3), 279–90.

Lopez-Real, F. and Chan, Y. P. R. (1999) Peer assessment of a group project in a primary mathematics education course. *Assessment and Evaluation in Higher Education*, 24 (1), 67–79.

Maki, P. (2004) *Assessing for Learning: Building a Sustainable Commitment across the Institution*. Sterling, VA: Stylus.

MacAlpine, J. (1999) Improving and encouraging peer assessment of student presentations. *Assessment and Evaluation in Higher Education*, 24(1), 15–25.

McDowell, L. and Sambell, K. (1999) The experience of innovative assessment: Student perspectives. In S. Brown and A. Glasner (Eds.), *Assessment Matters in Higher Education*. Maidenhead: SRHE and Open University Press.

Mentkowski, M. and Associates (2000) *Learning That Lasts: Integrating Learning, Development, and Performance in College and Beyond*. San Francisco: Jossey-Bass.

Nicol, D. and Macfarlane-Dick, D. (2006) Formative assessment and self-regulated learning: A model and seven principles of good feedback practice. *Studies in Higher Education*, 31(2), 199–218.

Ramsden, P. (2003) *Learning to Teach in Higher Education* (second edition). London: Routledge.

Sadler, R. (1989) Formative assessment and the design of instructional systems. *Instructional Science*, 18, 119–44.

Sivan, A. (2000) The implementation of peer assessment: An action research approach. *Assessment in Education*, 7(2), 193–213.

Tavner, A. (2005) Outcomes-based education in a university setting, *Australasian Journal of Engineering*, 2005. Retrieved 20April 2006, from http://www.aaee.com.au/journal/2005/tavner05.pdf

UGC (2005) *Education Quality Work: The Hong Kong Experience. A Handbook on Good Practices in Assuring and Improving Teaching and Learning Quality*. Hong Kong: University Grants Committee.